CW00660535

A complete guide to Lamping Rabbits with Lurchers

Philip Goss

Published Philip Goss, October 2021

ISBN: 978-1-8384967-8-4

Printed by
TJ Books Limited, Padstow

ACKNOWLEDGEMENTS

Frontispiece and chapter headings

Shaun Goss

www.shaungossart.com

Cover

David Rampling

www.ramplingart.co.uk

Thank you both for your help

DEDICATION

FOR NAN

Who always took such great delight in saying "stick that in your book, boy" while laughing aloud, convinced that I should write a book yet certain that I never would.

I have stuck it all in there, Nan.

INTRODUCTION

This book has been written with the intent of offering both an insight and guidance into the hugely exciting nocturnal method of taking (hunting) rabbits known as Lamping. I hope that it may guide new prospective Rabbit Lampers, offer perhaps an alternative system to more experienced exponents, whilst at the same time answering the many questions that someone with perhaps a milder, potentially non-active interest in our sport may have.

Most of all, I hope it acts as encouragement to any really determined individuals, people with a true passion for their sport, and to encourage them not to accept all they hear but to question, to push themselves harder and to help them form the absolutely essential close working relationship with their canine partner. Ultimately, having put in all of the necessary effort and shown the required level of commitment, I hope they are then suitably rewarded by achieving the absolute maximum from their sport in return.

It is hoped that this book will successfully fill a void and offer help to would-be lampers, particularly the young, in a way that was so badly missing for me. Whilst I have loved every moment of being out at night learning my trade, some well-intended practical advice from the beginning would certainly have been most welcome – it would have saved many mistakes from being made and prevented far too many lessons from being learnt the hard way.

To select the right puppy, to train it in preparation for what lies ahead and then to work with it successfully needs no greater reward in return. To step out at night, heading for ground that you know holds high numbers of rabbits, with a dog that you know is going to give you one hundred percent when you get there, is a feeling that as far as I am concerned has been unequalled in any other activity that I have pursued.

Lamping rabbits with a Lurcher is teamwork between man and dog – one cannot possibly be successful without the other, and the bond and working relationship that develops between you and your dog, the spectacle of the dog working, the excitement of each run, no two ever being the same, and the constant wondering of what the next field may hold, will keep you going long into the night.

It must be remembered that this book contains just one person's methods and opinions. These have been reached after over forty years' practical experience in the field; they are my opinions on how to get the most from our sport, a sport in which there are no rules. Others, I am certain, will have their own variations on how Lamping Rabbits with Lurchers should be conducted. I fully appreciate and respect the right for them to hold these opinions; however, these are my chosen methods, the ones that I use.

THE LAW

In 2004, the Hunting Act was passed, and whilst proving very restrictive to all working dog people, our quarry, the rabbit, was exempt.

The Schedule reads that:
The Hunting of Rabbits is exempt if it takes place on land –

[a] That belongs to the Hunter, or
[b] Which he has been given permission to use for the purpose by the occupier or, in the case of unoccupied land, by a person to whom it belongs

LIST OF ILLUSTRATIONS

Sire Jake 17

Dam Pure Greyhound 19

The long back that was important to the breeding project 19

Checking the front feet alignment 40

The type of front feet we are looking for 41

Good width of chest in proportion to size 42

Checking the back end 43

The type of back feet we are looking for 44

From the base of the neck we want the body shape to be rectangular, not square 45

Check the bite is true 46

Rumour at eight weeks, ticking all the boxes for me 49

Dreaming of long windy nights ahead 51

Lead training 63

Nothing seems to faze Rumour 63

Sit 68

Lie [down] 70

Stay [wait] 73

Walking to heel [back] 75

Retrieving at speed 79

Retrieving various objects....80

The sight we look forward to becoming accustomed to....82

Learning to jump at home....84

Jumping well within her capabilities....85

Jumping and retrieving combined and being carried out with confidence....86

22in Bearded Collie-cross trained by the author, who appears to have once had hair! Back in the early eighties clearing 8ft 4in....87

Rumour at four months old....91

Rumour....92

Shamus....93

Rumour at eight months old....94

Rumour at six months old....96

Simple but so effective slip lead....104

Ideal size and type of lamp, coiled cable taped to handle to provide additional protection against snagging and pulling cable out of light....106

Door-bell on/off switch....107

Purpose-made battery box, strong and wide webbing strap, industrial cable connectors compatible with either lamp, dependent on needs....108

Strings for bracing and aiding carriage....111

The body has hardened and the puppy is now equipped with the tools to do the job....120

Typical natural danger to a dog running the hedge at night................143

Important to be aware of these kinds of dangers before setting out at night 144

For me, too much danger in one area and the risk of injury or even worse is far too high. Despite this farm being lamped many, many times, this area is always avoided at night. Risk for reward does not add up...145

Why can't all hedges be like this? 151

The worst! The single strand wire leading straight into the wood. The greenery that at first glance appears to be a hedge is, in fact, rhododendron growing in the wood rooted about 8ft below the level of the field's surface – an absolute nightmare for the rabbit lamper – and any catch here is either very, very clever or very lucky. A place perhaps better revisited with a long net and keep the dog's confidence intact 152

Stone wall with the normal fallen stones creating a serious danger to the lamping dog 153

Nothing much stopping the rabbits running straight in here except a real brave and determined lunge which, with Whippet-type skin and the sharply angled gorse stems, could easily and often will lead to injury...................................154

Be sure to keep pressure true and in line with all limbs; dislocated legs will ruin presentation...182

The type of quality that will keep all outlets wanting more 183

CONTENTS

ACKNOWLEDGEMENTS v

DEDICATION vi

INTRODUCTION vii

THE LAW ix

LIST OF ILLUSTRATIONS .... xs

CHAPTER 1 – GETTING STARTED 1

CHAPTER 2 – KENNELLING AND DOG WELFARE 11

DIARY OF A LITTER (1) 17

CHAPTER 3 – SELECTION OF THE RIGHT PUPPY 21

DIARY OF A LITTER (2) 51

CHAPTER 4 – TRAINING 57

DIARY OF A LITTER (3) 90

CHAPTER 5 – EQUIPMENT 101

CHAPTER 6 – ENTERING 119

CHAPTER 7 – LAMPING 139

CHAPTER 8 – TAKING CARE OF THE CATCH 179

CHAPTER 9 – BREEDING 185

EPILOGUE 197

CHAPTER 1
GETTING STARTED

Lamping with Lurchers is a form of hunting conducted under the cloak of darkness by means of illuminating the quarry with artificial light. Having done so and identified a suitable target, the dog – normally a Lurcher – is then sent first of all to catch and then subsequently to gently retrieve to hand each individual rabbit.

This sounds easy enough – surely any fool could do that? The truth is, yes, they could; indeed, many fools do. However, perhaps not quite so many get as much from their sport as they could were they to put in the necessary preparation and effort to properly prepare both themselves and their dogs for the dark nights ahead.

Rabbiting in any form is usually exciting and very often rewarding, but surely Lamping with Lurchers has to be the most spectacular method of rabbit control of all. I would think that anybody who has been out Lamping with Lurchers, even those who have only ever seen it performed badly, are most unlikely to ever forget their experience.

How does someone become a Lamper? How does anybody become anything? Very often, we cannot remember what triggered any particular interest; sometimes it just seems as if it has always been there.

Personally, my interest in Rabbiting was initially restricted to ferreting. At that time I don't recall having any knowledge of Lurchers at all. Ferreting trips were very much group activities with mates, where often numbers of youths present outnumbered purse nets available. Needless to say, catches were few. Gradually, as we grew up, the friends with whom those special days were shared moved on to other pursuits, and ferreting trips became more and more single-handed and, it must be said, far more serious affairs.

Fate then played its part and a chance meeting with someone who had a Lurcher asked if I would like to accompany him on a day out ferreting where no nets would be used; instead, the rabbits would be bolted for his dogs to course. That was a very simple question to answer.

The day arrived, the ferrets went about their business, and soon a familiar sight of a bolting rabbit escaping across the field was had. This day, however, was different – the dog burst into action and the impossible gap between rabbit and dog closed in the blink of an eye and without any fuss a rabbit was in the bag. Those few seconds would prove to have an enormous influence on the course of my life. In addition to this long-term eventuality I had at that moment discovered what I needed to accompany me on my ferreting exploits in the short term. A Lurcher!

Immediately after this introduction to Lurchers, I would talk to anybody who would listen – and listen to anybody who could talk about them. I was fascinated by this recent discovery, and very soon this led to an invitation to a night's Lamping.

Lamping? What on earth was that? Anyhow, it wasn't long before, one dark windy night, I found myself in the back of a van, straddled by two muscular dogs intently staring down the headlights of the van as we twisted and bumped along the lane. I reached up and touched the back of one and was amazed at how solid it felt. Soon, we were out over the gate and the light went on. Whether we had permission to be there or not, I still don't know to this very day, but I had no intention of breaking the silence to ask a technicality such as that. I didn't know where to look – down the beam or at these two hugely impressive specimens. Suddenly, their expressions changed: a rabbit had been spotted, and one dog was released and the chase was on. All too soon it was over and the rabbit had been caught. I then discovered the real reason for my invitation and presence, as I was asked to run and get the rabbit, as the dogs didn't retrieve. This seemingly poor arrangement was perfectly acceptable to me, as I felt getting to spend time with these dogs meant that any chore in exchange still left me with the better deal.

Over the following months we had several excursions of this nature and I gradually started to appreciate some of the finer points of what was happening. One thing that became absolutely certain was that when I eventually acquired a dog of my own – and there was no question that I would be doing exactly that – its first lesson would be retrieving, because the novelty of running and fetching was by now wearing a bit thin.

Some nights would be spent seemingly endlessly getting in and out of the van for a run here and a run there. I would have preferred to just stay out and walk, but I had no right to any say in how the night should progress; instead, I just appreciated being there at all.

Later, lodgings were secured with a fittingly eccentric landlady on the single condition that I could build a kennel and keep a dog. This I did, and now found myself totally free to go out at night where and when I wanted and to go about it totally in whatever way I pleased. I very quickly developed a preference for being out alone and gradually, after what was perhaps a nervous start, learnt to keep my wits about me. I tried different ideas, learnt by my mistakes and came to realise that there was so much more to be had from lamping than was had from those earlier forays. That was over forty years and many nights lamping ago now, but I still remember that happy time as if it was yesterday.

So, my introduction to Lamping with Lurchers was in many ways opportunistic and not planned at all. I was very fortunate. In these modern times, however, I can imagine that for a lot of people things could easily work the other way around in knowing about Lurchers and being aware of lamping, but not having the opportunity to take their interest further before making any unnecessary commitment without at least a little first-hand experience.

Securing the opportunity of a night's lamping for anyone who personally knows someone who lamps should, of course, be relatively straightforward; but for those that don't, a bit more effort and research may be required. But whichever group a newcomer and prospective lamper falls into, I cannot emphasise enough how important I think this mentored introduction is at whatever the standard may be.

If you take up fishing and lose interest after a few trips, you just leave your rod in the garage and put the whole thing down to experience. To lamp with a Lurcher, it goes without saying you need a dog! For anyone acquiring a dog for the first time, it is a huge commitment and it would be unforgivable to just do so on a whim. If you cannot put in the effort to accompany someone else lamping for a while whilst you make sure that you really do want to take your interest further, at least for the dog's sake I would suggest that Lamping with Lurchers is not for you. Your dog is your partner, it is not a disposable item, and you owe it the opportunity to fulfil its potential and not end up overweight and lying on the settee, or worse.

How do you get yourself an invitation to go out lamping with someone? Whether you know them or not, the very nature of the beast would suggest that most lampers will be very reluctant to initiate or be bothered with someone who has nothing to offer in return. This is understandable, but there is the Achilles heel in their armoury: they may not want the bother and aggravation of your presence, but if you acquire some permission and invite them onto your ground, I can guarantee you will be greeted with a very different response.

When you have found someone prepared to take you out/come out with you, try to get out as many times as possible, and in those trips take in as much as possible. There will be a lot going on that would be easy to miss and could otherwise go unnoticed; and most importantly, be absolutely sure that you do indeed wish to become a lamper yourself.

A word of caution here would be that in succeeding with your quest for a lamping mentor, you will, of course, be placing yourself completely in their hands, and you could be forgiven for taking everything they say and do as gospel. There are, unfortunately, a lot of experts who have all the answers and yet no real experience; these people will stand and preach all day to someone who knows no better than to listen. These "pub lampers" will freely offer all sorts of advice to anyone prepared to keep the next pint coming; most would probably find it hard to find their way home from the pub, let alone going out into the field at night, so it goes without saying: do try to be a little careful in whose hands you place the future of your interest.

In reality, I think most lampers can be put into one of three main groups, although at times it is true that some may fall into all three groups, depending on what the independent occasion may demand and their objectives may be. However, the following are, I believe, a fair representation of the different groups.

Entertainment Lampers

This group, I am certain, would be by far the biggest. Within this group would be people who would perhaps rather take the dog out for a run with a nice supper the reward, rather than to stay at home and watch the television. Some may not even own a dog but may know someone who is happy for them to take theirs out; some may just permanently accompany someone else and just enjoy the exercise and spectacle when the mood takes them. For all of these people, the size of the bag at the end of the night would almost certainly be incidental and hold no real importance at all for many of them. Perhaps of greater importance would be that it doesn't rain whilst they are out. What is wrong with that? Nothing, as far as I am concerned, and who could deny that out walking at night is often a good time to put the world to rights in your own mind, and the exercise will not do any harm either.

Gamekeepers/Pest Controllers

This group, who may use their dogs for pest control, would take the night much more seriously, and where payment was being received for the job done, a casual approach would be most unacceptable. In situations where rabbit numbers had got out of hand, Lamping with Lurchers is more likely to be carried out in conjunction with other methods of control; and despite what your "pub lamper" may have told you, other methods at certain times in certain places are far more effective. Snaring and long nets will both bring down concentrated out-of-control numbers of rabbits very quickly;

although where these methods are utilised, there will still be a remainder that need removing, but whose numbers do not justify the use of either snare or net. Here the Lurcher has a role to play. Another example may be perhaps a market garden where even the smallest number of rabbits can have a disastrous effect on the produce, and here again the Lurcher may come to the fore, as it will in places where perhaps numbers are more thinly spread over a bigger area. In truth, Gamekeepers/Pest Controllers would be unlikely to keep a dog purely for rabbits – their dogs would more likely be versatile all-rounders and be expected to assist in a variety of tasks. Unlike the dogs owned by the third group.

Serious Rabbit Lampers

Here is the group who at various times the others will try to emulate. For these lampers, numbers are everything: they will not accept less than 100% from themselves or their dogs. This group of determined individuals will continue late into the night, long after the others are tucked up in bed. The importance of the weather is only for direction of wind and the phase of the moon; temperature is of no consequence unless it risks the feet of their canine partner on frozen ground, at which point proceedings stop, and rain is an occupational hazard hardly worth the mention.

These lampers are not jacks of all trades, they are specialists, and so are their dogs; they are out for rabbits – nothing more and nothing less – and as many as possible. These lampers would certainly be looking for the rewards of the night to equate to financial gain.

Many of this group will be poachers, because to lamp in this way requires a tremendous amount of ground to work; all will be labelled as such anyway – a peculiar Victorian sentiment that anyone who goes out regularly at night must learn to live with.

Anyone fortunate enough to make the acquaintance of someone from this group and be able to accompany them out at night will see just how adept their dogs become, how well man and dog complement each other, how they appear to know precisely what the other will do; they will notice how situations that are seemingly instantly assessed will bring positive results that far outnumber the negative.

If you are lucky enough to get out with one of this group, you are in for a treat, and any concern for permission to be on any particular piece of land will not be a factor for you if you have secured it yourself beforehand.

Anybody from one of these groups could help someone looking to start lamping. Obviously, someone from group three would be the best to learn from, but any would help you decide for certain that you want to take your interest further before you go ahead and consider acquiring a dog of your own. I bet over the years there have been some potentially outstanding dogs who, unfortunately, have fallen into the wrong hands and who have spent their lives unfulfilled. Your minimum aim must be to not add to this number.

After you have been out several times and find that you are still sure about starting up, you may like to consider what group you are likely to fall into yourself and realise how much it is all going to cost. Lamping dogs, even the worst, should be able to cover their own costs in time, but initially there is quite a financial outlay to prepare for, remembering that if you are wise and start with a pup, there will be a full twelve months before any sales money comes in.

Initially, you will have the price of the pup, closely followed by its inoculations. If the dog is to be kenneled, you will have already financed that; you will have food to provide for a year; and before you start lamping in your own right, you will require lamps and batteries, etc. Once your dog starts work, do not think it is all downhill, because, as with any athlete, injuries will occur and some may need veterinary attention; you must be ready for all of these additional expenses.

Your return for all this expense and effort will be the pleasure of working your own dog, and the bond that will build between you and any success you may achieve will bring enormous self-satisfaction of having achieved it all in the right way. Whatever group of lampers you ultimately fall into, your aim should be to have your dog trained and running to the highest standard possible, whether your intentions are to become the most serious of "serious lampers" or the most occasional of "entertainment lampers".

CHAPTER 2

KENNELLING AND DOG WELFARE

Having taken the decision to go ahead and acquire a pup of your own, before its arrival you are going to need to decide on where it will live. Will it be a kennel? Alternatively, some people prefer or just choose through ease to allow their dog to live in the house with them. As commendable as these intentions may be, my personal preference has always been to accommodate my working dogs outside in kennels. Having our dogs kenneled, of course, incurs additional expense at the onset, but later, when we return from a night's lamping and the dog is plastered in mud and soaking wet, we can easily rub it down with a towel and leave it to clean itself, without ruining the furniture and decoration in our homes. During the summer months, if the dogs are liberated from the kennel and free in the garden, they may still come into the house if they wanted to, with doors left open to permit it; however, you will normally find that even then they invariably choose and are happy to stay outside and sunbathe.

If, like me, your preference is to kennel your dogs outside, careful thought should be given to the type of construction chosen. You will, of course, need a good thick concrete pad to enable scrubbing down. I like to construct drainage within this pad and have at least a one or better still a two-block-high surrounding wall to contain all soiled cleaning water until it drains away and is deposited in the place of our choice, as opposed to seeping out randomly and polluting the surrounding area.

Probably borne through the amount of times I have moved house, from this point on when constructing a kennel I would recommend making the remainder sectional so that, if necessary, it can easily be dismantled and moved should the occasion arise.

It is worth considering before starting construction on your kennel the likelihood of a second or perhaps even a third dog taking up residence with you in the future; it is much easier and far more cost effective to make a single kennel big enough at the beginning than it would be to construct extensions later. If the prospect of additional dogs is a question that could not understandably be answered with any certainty at this moment in time, it could be worth at least bearing in mind before starting work. Perhaps your choice of design could be big enough to divide later, with features incorporated in this original construction intended to ease any alterations necessary later should they be required.

If you do eventually keep more than one dog and they are of opposite sexes, then, of course, at certain times of year they will need to be kept apart. Should a dog become injured, it may well appreciate being housed alone to recuperate, and these types of things are all worth considering now. The right decisions now, resulting in a well-constructed kennel, will give years of good service and provide comfortable accommodation for your canine partner/s.

Sleeping quarters do not need to be oversized, but like us in the morning, the bed wants to be at least big enough in either direction for your dog to stretch out fully. The run cannot be too big – that is impossible – but equally it doesn't need to be oversized, as it will not in any way contribute to any form of exercise. As long as it is big enough for the dog to lie out in the sun should the occasion present itself, without lying in its own mess, it will serve the purpose nicely. As a guide, and a guide only, I think eight foot square for a single dog to be a nice size. The sleeping quarters, of course, need to be roofed; that goes without saying, but my preference, in addition to this, would be for the whole construction to be roofed with wood and felt. Should you choose to not roof your run, provision will at least need to be made to contain the occupants, because, having taught your dog to jump, a six-foot side panel will not cause too much of a problem for them should they decide to jump over.

On the subject of possible escapes which could, depending on circumstances, easily lead to your dog becoming lost, make absolutely sure that your dog is micro-chipped and registered to you at your current address. It should be micro-chipped by its breeder by law before you purchase it, and you should receive appropriate documentation to change the ownership details into your own. If, for any reason, your puppy does not have this, get it done immediately; it is foolish not to, and if you care for your dog you will not think twice. Having got this security, if for any unfortunate reason you and your dog should become separated in the future, it will enable the appropriate people to contact you and reunite you with your dog.

Not all breeders will honour their responsibility of making sure that all of their pups have been chipped before they leave. This is annoying to us the buyers, but I wouldn't risk losing the right pup over it – we can always get it done ourselves. The best dogs don't always come from the best people. Inoculations are carried out at about ten weeks old, and though horribly expensive, we owe it to our dogs to get them protected. The alternative of not getting dogs inoculated is a horrible sight to see should you be unlucky and your dog becomes infected.

Feeding and Dog Maintenance

Feeding our dogs can very much be done on an individual trial basis, depending on how your dog responds to any certain brand of feed. A visit to any agricultural store will provide you with a whole range of complete diets to choose from. They are generally supplied in fifteen kilo bags. Someone new to the experience will wonder which food to choose – reading the information on the bags, they all sound so good. Of course, I am not a scientist, but it seems to me that all the modern-day complete diets appear to be of a perfectly acceptable and satisfactory standard for our dogs. The prices will range considerably; the higher priced ones, of course, will claim to be superior. I, like many other dog owners, am sure I have in the past used these expensive foods, believing that being full of good intentions I am doing the best I possibly can for my dogs, but in doing so I have not detected any noticeable difference in the well-being, stamina or energy levels of my dogs, and after doing the circuit of various well-known brands, now routinely feed my dogs on one of the relatively cheap brands that the dogs do equally well on and clearly enjoy as much as any. Dogs of the size that we keep will eat approximately 300-350 grams of food per day per dog on average, so a 15-kilo bag will last well over a month. They will need more when they are working hard and perhaps slightly less in the summer months. My dogs are routinely fed last thing at night so that should we go out lamping, they have not been fed, having their meal as soon as we get back. Feeding should be once a day only. Although the food is described as a complete diet, I also like to supplement it with regular fresh meat and bones which, as with all dogs, they really appreciate; on these fresh meat days I adjust the complete diet accordingly. A careful watch can be kept on your dog which enables you to monitor daily if it is either gaining or losing weight and, of course, in either scenario the appropriate action can then be taken.

In addition to a good well-balanced diet, I like to worm the dogs at three-monthly intervals after the age of three months, up until which time they will have been wormed fortnightly from birth on specialised puppy wormer. Also, every three months they get treated for exterior parasites by means of a drop-on liquid that you administer to the back of the neck where the dog can't reach to lick. This takes care of the majority of ticks, fleas and their like. Despite this careful regime, I would still recommend regular routine inspections, because whilst the treatment definitely helps keep pests at bay, it is also definitely not a one hundred percent guarantee that it will prevent them from minor outbreaks. Should this occur, the sooner you identify the problem, the easier it will be to eradicate it.

Another thing I would certainly like to advise, particularly when your dog starts work but as an overall general precaution, make sure your vet's telephone number is always at hand; hopefully you will never need it, but realistically, if you are going to work your dog regularly, it will get injuries from time to time. They may not necessarily be serious, but just in case they are, be prepared. Should your dog need immediate attention, the likelihood is that it will be late at night or in the early hours of the morning, and your vet may recommend leaving it until the following day, being reluctant to be disturbed at that hour. If you feel sure that your dog needs immediate help, don't take no for an answer, no matter what it costs you – your dog will have done its best for you, now you do your best for him/her.

I recall, several years back now, where one of my bitches had been running a rabbit that went underneath the gate of the field we were in and set off up the road. Soon after, the squeal of the rabbit betrayed the fact that it had been caught, so I went out into the road to collect it. As I flashed the light, I could see blood on the road, and when the dog returned to me, her tail had been spliced in two right down the centre. A single strand of barbed wire had been stretched across the bottom of the gate and somehow she had stood up after going under the raised gate, hot on the heels of the rabbit, and a barb had lodged into her tail near the base, unfortunately staying in there long enough to split her tail as she once again stood up fully and took off after the rabbit. The vet was immediately contacted as the blood loss was of real concern, but it turned out that the veterinary practice were having their Christmas party and though fortunately he had not been drinking, he was very reluctant to leave the festivities. Eventually, persuasion paid off and he did attend, and, seeing the wound, he quickly agreed that I had been right to insist, and even then with his resulting prompt action, he heavily doubted that the tail could be saved. Fortunately, the tail was saved, but well may not have been had the vet's initial response been accepted. Our dogs are dependent on us to act responsibly on their behalf at times such as this.

DIARY OF A LITTER (1)

The father of our most recent litter is a homebred 23in three-quarter Whippet/quarter Collie. He was the largest puppy in his litter of 10, something that was a factor when considering suitable mates for him. It was considered that it may be the right time to use a slightly taller bitch than what would usually be considered, given his ancestry, and having done so then hope to be able to select from the smaller puppies in the resulting litter.

Sire Jake

The sire "Jake" has excelled at Rabbit Lamping, but is now approaching his seventh year. His father, a pure Whippet, perhaps oversized for Whippet purists standing at 22in to the shoulder, was even better and the rabbit that had him behind it was in serious peril. So the paternal side of the prospective pairing inspired confidence.

On the maternal side, potentially suitable bitches available at home were close relatives of the father, and after a period of line breeding the family, it was decided, weighing up all the options, that perhaps the time had come to introduce fresh blood. I eventually decided to go back to a pure Greyhound; in doing so I accepted that there was always going to be a chance that the number of puppies of the desired size may be limited, but that concern was felt to be a compromise worth accepting in order to try and get the best from this particular sire.

The prospective mother of the pups was sought and eventually, after what proved to be quite an extensive search, a serious candidate presented herself.

We had contacted various Racing kennels throughout the country, always being perfectly open and honest of our intentions and specifying our requirements; several candidates were discussed, before a lengthy conversation with one particular racing breeder revealed that they had a three-year-old bitch that had just resumed racing after a long lay-off through injury. Despite all their best efforts, they were on the brink of accepting that this bitch may now never fully recover her former high standard. Eventually, it was agreed that if we waited until she had fulfilled her already arranged racing programme, we could have her. This we did, and were delighted with the outcome: she was a grade A1 middle-distance racer with a reputation for coming from behind. Well bred, she had tremendous conformation and, most importantly for us, she excelled in her back, which was the feature that I had already stated to all the potential vendors was of particular importance to us, as perhaps if Jake has a particular physical weakness, he could be longer in the back.

Dam Pure Greyhound

The long back that was important to the breeding project

CHAPTER 3

SELECTION OF THE RIGHT PUPPY

Having now been out on several lamping trips and enjoyed spending some time in the company of Lurcher people, you will have no doubt heard conversations regarding the merits of some dogs and the failings of others. There will be little doubt that these successes or failings will be attributed to the various breeds used in the genetic make-up and breeding of any individual specimen, and at this point it is doubtful that you will feel confident of knowing which way to turn when the actual moment arrives for you to obtain a puppy of your own. There is nothing to be ashamed of here, because if you have not realised by now you soon will that everyone has their own opinion of what constitutes the best rabbit lamping dog and how the best rabbit lamping dogs are produced.

In my opinion,which after all as is stated in the introduction to this book is all this book is, there is no such thing as the "ideal" rabbit lamping dog, and even if one should ever be or have been bred, the chances of it falling into the right hands and reaching its full potential by working on ground most suited to it are so remote that we may as well ignore this as any kind of realistic prospect.

There are so many variables in choosing the right puppy, particularly when that puppy has been crossbred, as, of course, all of ours are. The best we can do with this less than ideal set of circumstances is to attempt to narrow the chances into our own favour by stopping and thinking carefully before we take each step. Be assured you are in fine company, because nobody honest would claim to be able to identify from any litter at eight weeks old the puppy which later in maturity will excel at rabbit lamping; we can pick out the one that we think looks how we want it to look physically, but what nobody can see at this early stage or predict with any certain assurance is the true mentality of that particular pup. This will only reveal itself later in maturity when it is actually working. Thus, the mentality of the chosen specimen for me is the most important single factor that any working dog possesses, and this is what will ultimately make it stand out from the crowd. The pup with the right mentality, if that pup is even actually in our litter, may not necessarily be the one that appears most physically gifted; as in human behavior, it is not always the best-looking individuals who make the best workers. Yes, we can help any individual pup to develop, giving it every opportunity to fulfil its potential, but we cannot install that little extra if it is unfortunately missing right from the start.

However, there is a silver lining to every cloud, and for us it is that every Lurcher ever born will catch rabbits on the lamp, and enough to satisfy most owners. Very recently, I had a telephone call from someone living in a different part of the country who enquired if there would be any pups available any time soon. He was unknown to me and had obtained my number from someone else who had previously bought a pup from us in the past, and his very modest request was that he wanted a pup that would be guaranteed to catch half a dozen rabbits in a night on the lamp. I explained to him he would not have to travel far to find a Lurcher to meet his requirements because I have never in over forty years of lamping ever seen one that in normal circumstances couldn't do that.

So, with these positives and negatives in mind, we tread carefully forward. The mentor who has allowed you to accompany him may well be able to help you again in the acquisition of a pup. If you are certain he is the real deal and are sure that his dogs are the type you would like, this could be a simple and straightforward option. One thing to perhaps bear in mind at this early stage is that it is almost certain that someone not previously familiar with lamping dogs will be impressed by any that they see at work, so do be sure that this mentor can genuinely help you progress. A further word of warning here perhaps is that when the word goes around that someone is looking for a lamping dog, it is quite likely that one, a world beater, will miraculously arrive on your doorstep. My advice would always be to start with a pup. Resist temptation. You will not be going out lamping alone with your own dog immediately, but when you eventually do, the pleasure of having done things the right way and the bond that will have developed between you and your dog will more than make up for having to be patient at the outset. You will become familiar with your dog's ways, he/she will become familiar with yours, and you will not have to spend the following winter cursing the person who sold you the world beater when its deficiencies inevitably come to light.

In this modern day, at any one time there are literally hundreds of litters of Lurcher pups available. Each litter will have their claim to fame and each litter will be invariably described as "stunners" – that seems to be the most frequently used modern description. Being a dinosaur, I remember a time when the few litters that you may become aware of were likely to have a selling point such as "both parents live to hand" to accompany them; you never see that any more. Presumably that no longer counts, or perhaps more likely I think is the sad prospect that many of the litters produced these days are from dogs that are unproven in the field.

The popularity of the Lurcher in comparison to years ago is unquestionable, and I assume that some of these available litters may have to go back several generations before a real working ancestor is found. Some of the sundry breeds of dogs included in some of these modern day "Lurcher" litters mystify me, as I cannot see what they can possibly bring to the table or what the need is for their inclusion other than perhaps a fluffy coat or a pretty colour – literally the last thing that anyone looking for a working Lurcher should care about.

Anyway, dismissing the above as of no interest to us, where does that leave a genuine person looking for a prospective genuine rabbit lamping dog? I see no value in aiming low, even if from the concept a person who was expecting to become an occasional entertainment lamper and no more, why not spend your money, time and effort on a dog that is truly fit for purpose and a dog to be genuinely proud of?

The starting point for any type of Lurcher, whether it is wanted as an all-rounder or as, in our case, a specialist, has to come from the group of dogs known collectively as sighthounds – with these dogs just a quick glance will tell you they are built for speed and as the name suggests, rely on sight when hunting. They are quite a big group with a variety of breeds for us to consider, but I think that there are only four of genuine interest to the serious Lurcher breeder. Remembering that opinions on these breeds are based on the working/racing type specimens, not their show-related cousins which appear to have left the aforementioned and much quoted phrase "fit for purpose" some way in their distant past, we will leave them for others, as they hold no interest for us.

The Deerhound

The Deerhound is, for me, a tremendously impressive creature. I like them a lot. Of particular importance to the Lurcher breeder can be their size, at around twenty-eight to thirty inches to the shoulder, as can their beautiful protective rough coat. However, what we are looking for is a rabbit specialist, and as beautiful a creature that a Deerhound undoubtedly is and as useful as it unquestionably would be for those with other interests, it is also quite clear that this animal was not produced to hunt rabbits – it is quite simply too big for us. People will read this, I am sure, and have names of individual dogs who regularly catch rabbits, and, of course, Deerhounds do. I have also caught rabbits with pure and first-cross Deerhounds, but they cannot be expected to match the capabilities in this discipline of other more suitably sized sighthounds. Remember, what we are trying to do is narrow the odds to our favour in securing the dog we require; using a breed that is clearly oversized for our needs cannot be the right place to start.

The Saluki

Again, a wonderful-looking animal that, along with its Greyhound hybrid, used to find fanatical support in Hare Coursing circles. Those days have sadly passed now, but the capabilities of these graceful dogs lives on in our memories. Salukis are known for, in many cases, having better stamina than most of their other sighthound counterparts, and they also have a tendency to have strong feet, with knocked-up toes being far less common. Two beneficial attributes to any rabbit lamping Lurcher, and it is certain that these traits would not go unnoticed to the rabbiting man. We all have moments that have a fundamental effect on one's opinions, and for me, watching a pure Saluki course a hare (pre-ban) without ever really pushing itself, bit deep into the core; the course went on and on, and in fairness to the dog, he caught his target, although to this day in my mind I question whether the dog caught the hare or just simply outlasted it.

Of course, not all Salukis run like this, but many can run hot and cold. Once again, for us rabbit lampers, basing our Lurcher on a dog who could blow hot and cold when there is no need to, I think is at best a questionable action and one for us to perhaps avoid.

The Greyhound

The Greyhound – what a dog! Fast, strong, fearless and determined to the point of obsessed with the thrill of the chase. This breed has so much to offer any Lurcher enthusiast wanting to breed any type of Lurcher. Unfortunately, there are always drawbacks: size, in its pure form a greyhound is too big for the "ideal" rabbit dog; stamina, another important requirement in our lamping dogs, is also sadly lacking in a Greyhound; the ability to maintain its exceptional speed and the recovery time between runs is not what we are looking for. Again, I have lamped with fit, pure Greyhounds, and whilst they all proved perfectly capable of picking up rabbits and having qualities that we clearly desire in our lamping dogs, they also all revealed their limitations. So, whilst a Greyhound perhaps offers us more than the Deerhound or the Saluki, it would certainly not be enough on its own to satisfy our requirements.

The Whippet

Here we have a sighthound with which the use of in the production of Rabbit Lamping Lurchers is unquestionable right from the start. The Whippet's agility, due in no small part to its diminutive size, is second to none. Its top speed, whilst not matching that of the Greyhound, is more than fast enough for what we require, but perhaps of more importance to us is the time it takes to attain top speed – the acceleration a whippet can show is incredible. Despite their size, Whippets are tough little dogs and can stand up to many of the rigours of a night's rabbit lamping. Drawbacks once again: size is a concern, only this time for the opposite reason – Whippets are just too small; the catching ability of these little dogs is unquestionable, but it seems to me that the effort each run and subsequent retrieve demands taxes the strength of such a small dog, and tiredness encourages any dog to become a prematurely hardmouthed, something that a serious Rabbit Lamper hoping to sell their catch would want to avoid at all costs. Once again, I sense arms being thrown up as people have examples of how this sentiment is unfounded; exceptions do and always will occur, but in my experience this is a fair appraisal. The last pure whippet that I ran regularly was the grandfather of the litter ("Diary of a Litter" that runs through this book), and I had nothing but admiration for him and pitied the poor rabbit that he got behind; his strike rate was phenomenal, but true to his type, despite his remarkable success, he had his ancestral limitations. Skin type in Whippets can also often be a problem: many Whippets have very thin skin, and whilst I have heard of Whippets that bounce off a barbed-wire fence, I have never owned or seen one. Barbed-wire and Whippet skin has invariably and all too often resulted in vets' fees and, much more importantly, a dog out of action for me. Like it or not, pure Whippets unfortunately, despite their obvious merits, also have their physical limitations.

So there are our four main breed candidates from the sighthound family which could comfortably form the base for a working Lurcher of any type. What we are looking for is a specialist, and because of this I believe that only two of these four have realistic value in our quest: the Greyhound and the Whippet, accepting that neither of these two breeds in their pure form are exactly what we want. What if we crossed the two together? Although we would have no guarantee of the precise level of physical inheritance, I believe that a pup of this breeding that fell between the two in terms of size should be a step in the right direction and should and almost certainly would prove to be a noticeable improvement on either parent; in fact, if we remain optimistic and suggest that the pups inherit their agility and acceleration from the Whippet and the top speed and determination from the Greyhound, we would be well on our way. Logically, however, even allowing for hybrid vigour, the full amount of improvement required would unfortunately not be achieved from this alliance alone. Tractability, stamina, robustness a general overall ability to take all the knocks and bumps that a lamping dog must endure, are sadly not improved by this pairing. Neither is what would be at the very top of my personal wish list: thick skin. A lot is made of the protection a dog receives from a rough coat, and to a degree this has to be true, but give me thicker skin every time; a rough coat on thick skin would surely be the best, if only it was that easy to achieve. So, whilst the Greyhound and the Whippet undoubtedly have a part to play in the production of our Lamping dogs, alone or combined they leave unacceptable weaknesses that we are going to need a third breed – clearly not a sighthound – to rectify for us.

Now we enter a minefield, as the chances of two breeds producing uniform and predictable results are very slim, before we even contemplate adding a third; but a third we must, for I genuinely believe that if we are going to strive for perfection whilst realistically accepting we are most unlikely to ever achieve it, then we have to include a breed that can correct our previously identified failings, we can satisfy ourselves that each step we take along the way the puppies produced should always be improvements on their parents, and as such will more than satisfy the needs of most.

At this point, I also think it worth mentioning the vast number of non-sighthound breeds used in modern day "Lurcher" production by various people for various, sometimes impossible-to-see reasons; some, I suppose, it could be argued make sense; some, unfortunately, make no sense at all. It is clear that the Lurcher has long since just been the working dog that it once was, but why people feel the need to produce puppies that are never going to have a hope of excelling or even be useful in any of the myriad of tasks asked of a true Lurcher, is beyond me. So, for a newcomer to our sport, my recommendation would be to ignore the novelty litters and stick to the proven breeds that have been tried and successfully tested for use in Working Lurcher production. One final, perhaps contradictory, thought on this matter, however, is that you see all sorts of nonsense litters, from huskies, pointers and goodness knows what, yet I have never seen an advert for a Labrador-cross which, in my mind, if you really did have to go outside the box, has on paper at least much to offer – presumably the offspring wouldn't be pretty enough! Enough said.

The list of our outstanding requirements only points us in one direction: the Collie. There are many Terrier-cross enthusiasts, particularly those who work Bedlington and Bull-cross hybrids, who will disagree and argue their corner, and they are perfectly entitled to have their own opinion. Many who know me personally may even perhaps be surprised by this statement, as I have dogs that have Bull blood running through their veins in my kennel; all take rabbit on a regular basis, but none would contribute in my mind to the production of a Rabbit Lamping specialist. When we are catching and selling large numbers of rabbits, we have a duty to consider the quality of the produce we provide, and anyone who doesn't will eventually run out of outlets prepared to take their hard-earned catches. Terriers were not created to be softmouthed; despite this, yes, some can be, but for how long? You cannot fault them for effort; in fact, effort is often their undoing by way of not being able to find reverse gear; but as much as I admire this trait and personally appreciate Terrier-cross capabilities in other fields, there is no need for us to include them in our own Rabbiting dog mix, as we have a very clear objective to aim for here and the addition of extra unnecessary and frankly unwanted ingredients makes no sense.

If you were making a cake and knew the ingredients you required but had no scales available to correctly calculate amounts used, you could still go ahead and estimate what you put in; doing so, you would probably still end up with something close to the cake you were looking for. However, if you started throwing in a bit of this and a bit of that in disregard, it is a certainty that you would not end up with anything like what you were hoping for. So it is for us: we are looking for a specialist – any breed whose strengths and qualities don't either take us in the right direction and/or compensate for weaknesses in the other breeds used are eliminated from our mix. So, accepting the wrath of all Terrier enthusiasts, I can only recommend the use of the Collie along with the Greyhound and Whippet in attempting to create our perfect partner.

The Collie for me fills all the voids, ticks all the boxes and leaves no reason to look any further – we have all that we need wrapped up in one suitably sized breed. Unfortunately, working out what we need on paper is quite simple in comparison with trying to blend them successfully into a single individual specimen, and it must be remembered that within any of our three chosen pure breeds there is a level of variation both genetical and regional, so which individual specimens we select to use becomes vitally important; for example, there are Collies and then there are Collies. One example of a Border Collie that always springs to my mind I came across whilst working in Scotland. He was very tall, in keeping with the hill work that he primarily did, was very strong and had stamina to the point of disbelief. He appeared to know exactly what was required of him at any given time and in addition to all of his farm work, one of the three farming brothers who he worked with used to lamp rabbits with him quite regularly, and he had some pretty impressive tallies to his name, which, knowing this particular dog, was of no great surprise. This dog seemingly never slept. He was the only dog on the farm and it appeared that his services were constantly in demand by one brother or the other, and I honestly never saw that dog tired. This is the Collie for us, the one that has truly proven that he has what it takes and, perhaps more importantly, what we need. We cannot possibly expect the Collie we see on a Sunday morning walking around the park with an old lady to help us in the same way; it may do, of course, who knows? But why take the risk? Only use the best, and what has been proven to be the best; we have to remain focussed and sensible in our choices in order to continue narrowing the chances to our own favour. My preference has always been for using the Border Collie, but that as much as anything has certainly been influenced by the shortage of genuine working-type Bearded Collies available. I have used Bearded-crosses and in truth, if there is a difference in mentality, I haven't been able to detect it. The Bearded-crosses can inherit a rough coat which tends to be very attractive and useful, but the type of Collie for me should always be the best available, and this, due in no short measure to their abundance, has invariably been the Borders.

I genuinely believe that the right blend of these three breeds – the Collie, the Greyhound and the Whippet – in the right proportions, both physically and mentally, reared properly, trained and entered in the correct way on any type of terrain, and given time to learn its trade by someone who understands their own role and who respects their canine partner, together would prove unbeatable. For all those factors to fall into place is most unlikely, but it is what we are aiming for. The human aspect should be simple: if you can't put in the effort, you don't deserve to succeed. Anyway, the most difficult part in this equation will be to find exactly the right blend in your puppy.

The starting point for attempting our project would be to fully understand and be clear of our true objective, whilst at all times accepting and understanding that the road ahead will be full of compromise. Puppies produced along the way will all have potential and all deserve the effort to be put into them in order that they should fulfil it, whilst never losing sight of the ultimate goal that, unless we are extremely lucky, we have accepted perfection may never be achieved.

What would be the perfect blend? In a perfect world, my intention in trying to produce the "ideal" Rabbit Lamping Lurcher would be to breed litters where the expected average size to the shoulder was in the region of twenty-three inches. This, I believe to be the perfect size for the job we have for them; you would hope that if you crossed a dog of twenty-four inches to a bitch of twenty-two, then all the puppies should be twenty-three – simple! Wrong already. Prepare yourself for the first compromise: Lurcher breeding is never that simple. All we can do is remain connected to our quest and think carefully in trying to make the right choices for the right reasons.

The starting point for me would be to pair a Whippet to a Greyhound; the resulting puppies should all be an improvement on either parent for what we want them to do and should prove quite capable. Unfortunately, as skilful as they will almost certainly prove to be, they will also have severe limitations if we are aiming for the ultimate individual dog. Whippet/Greyhounds will invariably have a very high strike rate, but for a limited time only. Obviously, the fitter they are, the longer the nights can go on, but all will be found wanting if your intention is for a long night and a big bag. Perhaps we could overcome these deficiencies by having more than one dog and by running a team? You could (and I have) bring out a fresh dog when the first starts to tire, but your solution will prove to be disappointingly short-lived as if you run like this regularly, the next problem we find with this first-cross hybrid will inevitably rear its ugly head when injuries start to occur and gradually your team will initially be partially and subsequently completely depleted. No, this first-cross, as commendable as it is for us, must be a stepping stone in the right direction; a puppy of this breeding can initially be used successfully within its capabilities, but more importantly, it offers us huge breeding potential for the future whilst also being able to fill a role as a back-up dog later as we progress.

Having secured, tried and tested our Whippet/Greyhound and still confidently marching forward, we now need an infusion of Collie blood. I would not recommend the obvious here, as pairing to a straight Collie would give us too strong a dose, and despite the Collie blood being a godsend and a genuine game changer, unlike the saying, I believe in at least this instance you can, in fact, have too much of a good thing. I would never recommend the use of a full Collie as a parent. I have done it and paid the price. Nor would I recommend the alliance between two dogs carrying Collie blood. Both of these two options for me carry the higher risk of having too much Collie blood in our dogs – risks that, having learnt the lessons the hard way, I would never want to take again and would not recommend anyone else like-minded to take.

I am fully aware of the level of support that a first-cross Collie/ Greyhound may find in the Lurcher fraternity, and all I can say to those people is good luck, this cross may well be the ultimate jack of all trades, as it is reputed to be, but personally I heavily doubt it, and beyond that, we are not in any case looking for a jack of all trades – we are looking for a specialist. I accept that I am talking very broadly and exceptions have, do and always will occur, but whenever I have worked dogs with a proportionately high dose of Collie blood, over a sustained period they start to develop the same infuriating traits: picking their runs, deciding for themselves which rabbits they can and can't catch. I have had heavily Collie-blooded dogs run ten yards, decide that this run was not for them and give up; then the same dog a minute later would crash through a hedge to prevent an escaping rabbit as if their life depended on it. This inconsistency to me is totally unacceptable. I cannot be doing with that; the lamper should be able to decide which and when a rabbit is run. I prefer the dog to concentrate on its own job. A lamping dog should be able to be relied upon to give one hundred percent at all times, no matter what the odds. We can help encourage this attitude by being sensible on what we ask from our dogs and never abusing the effort our dogs are prepared to apply. Be fair, and while understanding that every rabbit is potentially catchable, we must not continuously send the dogs for runs that are almost certain to end fruitless and in doing so affect our partner's confidence – a confident dog is the very attitude we need to instil, develop and retain in our dogs at all costs. I have not encountered these problems in dogs with a lower concentration of Collie blood; yes, it would be fair to say that these to us more favourable specimens were perhaps not quite so intelligent, but that's okay, we can work with that if that is what it takes. People may be inclined to think that a dog knowing its limitations should be beneficial. Why run a rabbit it knows it can't catch?

My point exactly – it doesn't know it can't catch it! I have seen rabbits carry out remarkably clever moves to avoid capture in what were seemingly impossible situations; equally, I have seen rabbits do crazy things that have really equated to suicide when escape seemed inevitable and a formality. So, in order to help preserve our own individual roles, a more diluted dose of Collie blood is required to be partnered with a lamper who respects his dog.

How to achieve this specialised blend is delicate, but I think if you aim for no more than twenty-five percent Collie in your mix, in my experience this is much safer territory. I have never experienced the aforementioned problems with dogs of this breeding, but have certainly benefited from the Collie's inclusion. There are several different ways of achieving this blend, e.g.

Collie/Greyhound x Greyhound/Whippet
Collie/Whippet x Greyhound/Whippet
Collie/Greyhound x Whippet
Collie/Whippet x Greyhound

Any of these examples – providing they were genuinely what is stated – would excite me in a search for the best starting point for a Rabitting Lamping Lurcher. Mates for individual specimens would, of course, be selected for size, always trying to stay on or near to the twenty-three inch to the shoulder mark. If size was in doubt, I would always opt for the slightly too big as opposed to the slightly too small; to me that interprets to perhaps a slightly lower yield of rabbits, but a yield more likely to remain undamaged. As I have said, compromise is very much the name of the game in our inexact science. If the right size Pure Whippet for us is used – which basically means one that is oversized according to the aficionados – then a three-quarter Whippet/Collie (Whippet x Whippet/Collie) could suffice, but normally this cross would result in an unacceptably high percentage of offspring being below the size we are looking for, and so unacceptably restricts the choice of really useful specimens available to us.

In future breeding, again always try to maximise the majority of offspring at around the twenty-three inch mark. It may be deemed appropriate to reduce the level of Collie blood further; I would certainly rather have too little than too much, but would always want to keep the Collie's input. One eighth would be the minimum; I would not want to reduce any further.

Although we must accept that it is very much a matter of both chance and luck as to whether we actually get all the right attributes from our selected breeds wrapped up in one dog, it can be seen by using the breeds that excel in our requirements we have got to have shortened the odds significantly in our favour. I think for any type of Rabbit Lamper, from entertainment through pest control to the most serious of serious Rabbit Lampers, these dogs will match the requirements admirably. I would certainly not be so narrow-minded as to try and suggest that this type of dog is the only type that could make first class Rabbit Lampers, but what I would say is that an average dog of this breeding would leave the others wanting in our chosen pursuit. If you were fortunate enough to get a really good one, others may match it, but very few will ever better it.

Having decided exactly what we want, it will now be found that this calculation was the simple part in comparison to securing the genuine article. One massive improvement in this modern era is how simple the search for what you want is in comparison to pre-internet days: you can now easily look through the adverts, rushing past the Husky-crosses, Pointer-crosses and their ilk. Do not settle for anything other than what you want. They will be there; you may have to wait and you may have to travel, but if you are not prepared for either, your heart may not be completely in what you are doing. Hopefully you won't have to, but if you do – you do. You may even travel a long distance only to find on arrival that the pups are not what they were advertised to be or have clearly not been reared to the standard that they should have been, so a fair appraisal of them is simply not possible. Walk (or drive) away – do not settle for anything other than exactly what you have decided on.

Let's remain optimistic. You have found a litter and your enquiry has been well received, and better still, you have been offered a choice, perhaps even the pick of the litter! Where do we start?

Are both parents available to see? Hopefully so. The mother, of course, will be – remember, she has just had a litter, so she can be forgiven for not looking at her best – but nevertheless, she can still be inspected. Even if you don't feel comfortable carrying out a full inspection of her due to her obvious condition, you can assess her as you talk to the vendor. If the father of the pups is not available to see, you can be sure at least pictures will be. Remembering that you are under no obligation to buy, walk away if anything does not meet the standard you are looking for or does not feel right. Incidentally, if you should for any reason doubt that you have found what you are looking for, do not be swayed by a sudden reduction in price if the seller senses you are not happy with what you see. If that happened, I would definitely walk away immediately. Equally, the price for the puppy will have been advertised and known before your visit, so don't make the senseless mistake of offering less and trying to haggle; if you are not happy with the price, don't even go and look. I have had people apply for puppies and when they did become available, the buyer would start trying to haggle. Those people don't buy puppies from me. Some have subsequently come back and offered more than the original asking price to try and secure one, but that ship has sailed – they don't get one from here. If you are going to jib over £20 or so, what are you going to do when the dog needs your financial support, perhaps through injury? The price of the puppy is not important, the quality of the pup is; and let's be honest, the price of a Lurcher pup, no matter how extravagant it may be, is not likely to be out of anyone's reach if they genuinely want one.

Hopefully, all is well: the price we know in advance, the Dam and the Sire look in good order and appear to be exactly what it was claimed they were. So now to the pups. Every puppy ever born is a sweet little thing, and Lurcher puppies are no exception, and with the variety of colours you could easily be sucked in, so stay focused. When you finally decide you have found the pup you want, this decision will be the biggest you will make. From that point on, this is the pup you will be training and potentially working with for several years to come, so do not be rushed, bullied or swayed into doing anything except exactly what you want to do. Take your time.

Let's assume that we have the pick of the litter. The sex of the puppy is the first possible restriction: will this puppy be involved in any already-started breeding project in addition to its main purpose; will it eventually perhaps be kennelled with other dogs? If so, then this may immediately restrict our choice. Again, let's assume that we are not restricted by any of these considerations. Dogs have a tendency, but no more, to be bigger than their sisters, but you get big bitches and you get small dogs. If the parents are on the slightly big size, you may pay more attention to the smaller pups, and vice versa, but make sure you look at them all. The first thing is to look at them as a group: are they all full of it? Hopefully they are. Are there any signs of nervousness? We don't want that. Do they look like they have been well reared, clean and healthy? Are they plump without being fat? Have they been regularly wormed? Have they been correctly weaned from their mother? These are all points to initially assess.

Satisfied that all is in order, at this point I always stand back and watch each pup individually to start with and try to pick out any that I think may be of less interest, for what ever reason. The longer this takes the better, as if you have to search for something wrong then we are on the right track. Try to reduce the number to perhaps four and then give these four a more thorough inspection. At all times we have to remember that they are just weeks old and they are going to change so much in the coming months; but, at seven to eight weeks old, there will be strong indicators present as to the quality of each individual pup. As you look at them, place a hand under the ribcage and gently lift their front feet off the ground, looking from over their heads. Are their feet facing directly away at twelve o'clock, or are they pointing at five to one (or worse)? Anything other than twelve o'clock is not what we are looking for. I have kept pups in the hope that their feet will grow out straight, but they never do. This is a flaw. Do the feet have toes that are nicely boxed? For example, looking from the side, do they look like an upside down L or are they flat-footed? You don't want the toes exaggeratedly boxed, but this angle provides a type of shock absorber later when the dog is running, and God knows, our dogs need that when they start work. Flat feet is a definite no thank you, so walk away. Five to one feet with nice toes is not ideal, but still worth carrying on the inspection – but do remember that all the pups share the same genes, so any faults that a discarded pup may carry are likely to be carried by each sibling, even if that sibling doesn't show them. This may be an important factor in consideration for any future breeding plans.

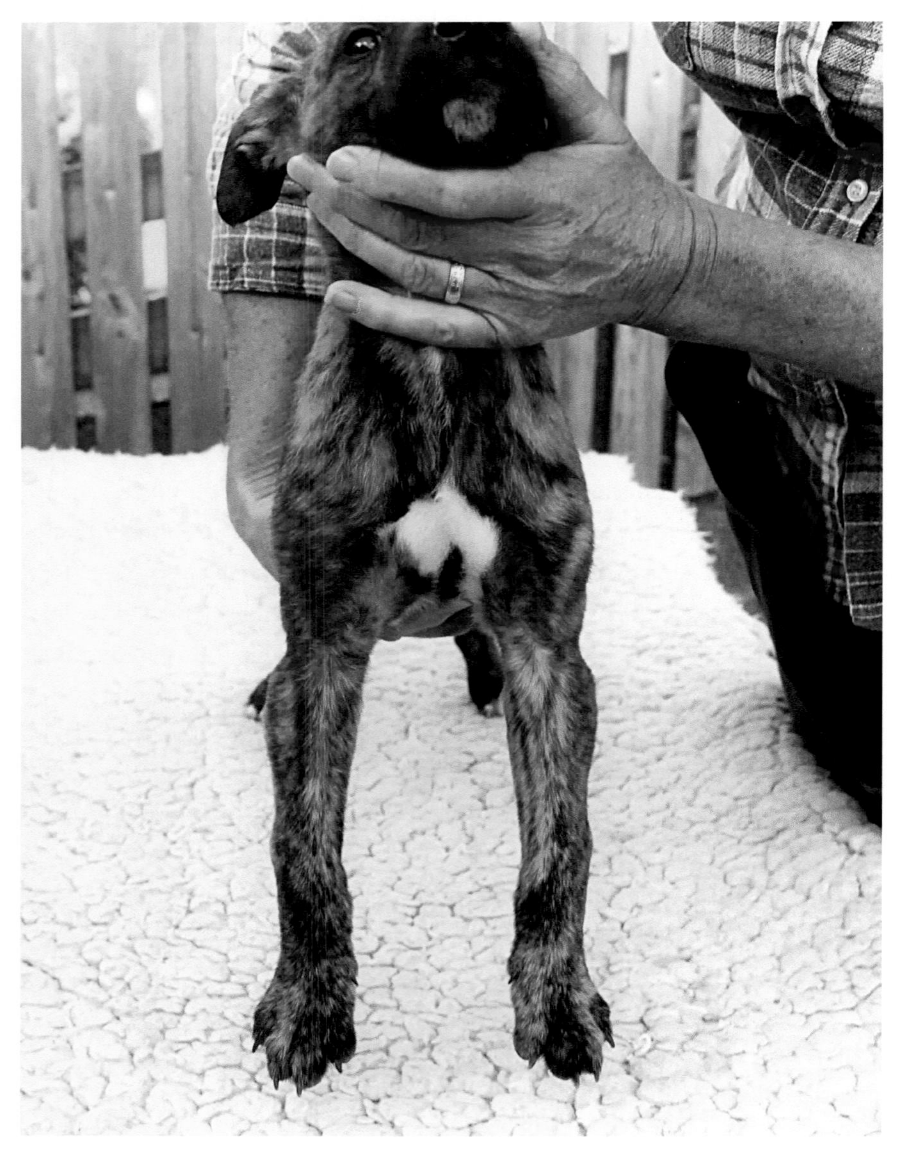

Checking the front feet alignment

The type of front feet we are looking for

See if it can be arranged to have some sort of table arrangement put in place so that you can stand them up and easily get down to their level – a dustbin with the lid replaced by a piece of board and covered with a piece of carpet will do nicely. Stand them facing you. We know about their front feet – have they got width between the top of the front legs? A narrow chest, as well as harbouring potential internal restrictions, can be the root cause of other external easy-to-diagnose defects, including feet facing at five to one. Albeit indirectly, a narrow chest can pull in the elbows that in turn will influence the carriage of the legs and, of course, in turn the feet. They should have a nice width of chest supporting strong legs, which should be as straight as possible.

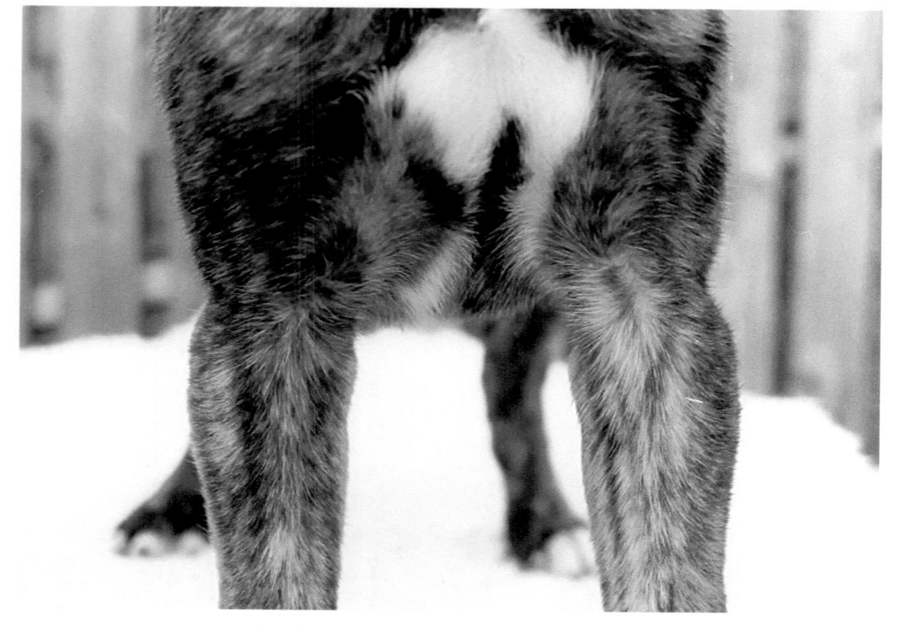

Good width of chest in proportion to size

They will show knuckle at what we call the knee, but that is normal and will grow out. Assuming that we are still happy, turn them around and start looking at the back end. If the pup starts to fidget, let it go down. We have only selected four to inspect in this way, so if necessary we can do front ends first and back ends second; with only four, we will easily remember what we had previously found.

With the pup facing directly away, gently place your hand between the back legs, with the tail in the palm of your hand, and take the weight off the feet. Then place them gently down and watch as the legs resume taking the pressure. Do they stay straight as you would like them, or do the hocks bend in?

Checking the back end

Hocks bending inwards is not what we require, and depending on the level of severity, it should not be ignored, although again we must allow for the tender age of the pups – at eight weeks old, the hocks should ideally remain straight when viewed from directly behind. Standing the puppy sideways on, we can first of all check the back feet. If the hocks were indeed bending in, then you can be almost certain the feet will be pointing out. The angle of this imperfection will suggest how badly affected the puppy is. Should the feet be straight, despite the concern on the hocks, I would be happy to leave the puppy in contention; but if they are not and the problem appears to be more severe, I would eliminate that pup from contention at this point.

The type of back feet we are looking for

Assuming we are still satisfied with what we are finding, whilst the puppy is still sideways on, we can observe the length of its back. I always like a puppy whose basic outline from the base of the neck backwards resembles a rectangle; this suggests a satisfactory length of back. A puppy with a square outline, for me, would be showing a short back.

From the base of the neck we want the body shape to be rectangular, not square

It could be argued that it has long legs, but call it what you will – and I call it short in the back – for me it has to be rectangular or nothing at this age; its length of back will later in life dictate the length of stride, and for me these puppies invariably mature into more balanced specimens. If all of the previously mentioned checks were satisfactory, I would start to feel encouraged, as these characteristics are the most important to us at this age.

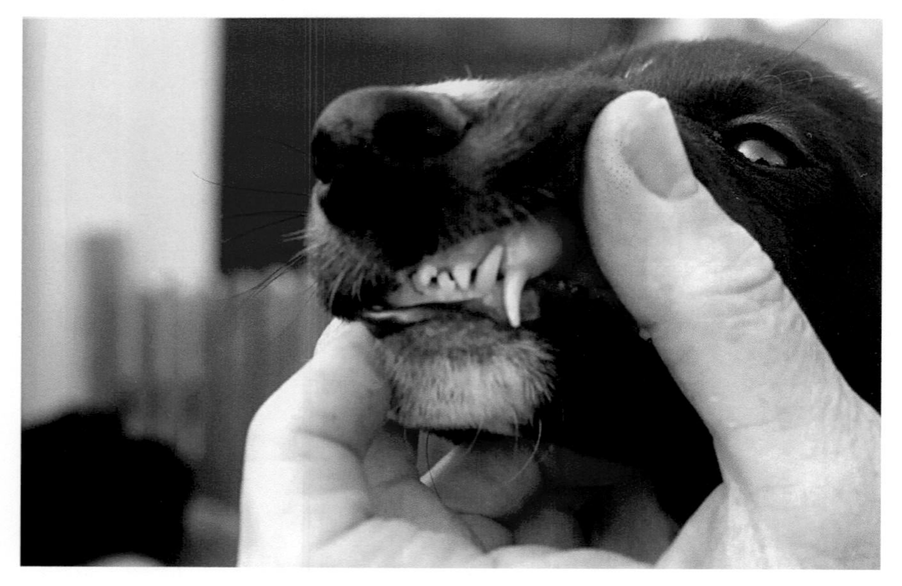

Check the bite is true

Ideally, the pup would have a good mouth, with the jaws shutting together correctly, and it would carry its tail in a pleasing manner to accompany its more important structural features, but these factors are more the icing on the cake rather than anything to be overly concerned about at this stage, as is the colour. We all have our favourites, but colour is unimportant – it does not make the slightest difference to the dog's ability what colour it is. On the subject of colour, many poachers would not welcome a white-bodied dog, believing that it would stand out too much should they be where they should not be. Having encountered many illegal lampers during my keepering career, more often than not, on such occasions it was the glint reflection from the dog's eyes in my lamp that gave the poacher's whereabouts away, any colour on the dog only becoming clearer at a much closer range. Had they covered the dog's eyes, they may well have remained undetected. I once ran a bitch who had a face and neck that were very precisely divided half black and half white – at and beyond a certain range she was much easier to follow with the lamp on her white side than her black, but under most circumstances colour really doesn't matter.

It is most likely that this thorough inspection will have eliminated perhaps one or two more of the puppies and leave just the cream to select from. Having made your choice, be sure you haven't missed anything, and put the preferred pup to one side for a moment. Just as a final check, take a last look at the puppies you originally dismissed and be sure you haven't made a mistake and missed one. Also, any from the four more thoroughly checked pups, double-check the flaws that caused you to eliminate them and try to be sure you were indeed correct and the faults are of genuine concern.

You may find that the vendor advises you that you will not find anything wrong with any of the pups as you inspect them. Well, that is good news, as in this case he shouldn't mind you checking if he has nothing to hide. You should never be critical of any of his pups that you do not favour; just politely state that this is not the pup for you and continue your inspection of the others. The pup you are searching for is, we hope, in the future going to grow into a supreme athlete; in order to achieve this status, it will need all its features in the right place, facing the right way and working smoothly together. Just as in a car which has unbalanced wheels, you should expect the tyres to wear out prematurely, unevenly or perhaps both; likewise, if the engine components are not aligned, you are not going to get far before you encounter problems. Your dog must have everything working together as smoothly as possible. In adult form you can get a very strong indication of the conformation of a running dog just by watching it move. For those with perfect conformation, when they run it all appears so easy for them, they move effortlessly, everything is fluid and free; those with less than perfect conformation will have their own individual running styles, which will very likely be jerky, full of effort, uneven and generally awkward, and we do not want that. To be successful in adult life, our pups are going to need every little bit of help available. The job they are bred for and destined to do is one that they will love, but also one that will very quickly expose any weaknesses. We cannot be absolutely certain at this early stage, but we can take every precaution available to try and avoid anything unwanted like that happening to us.

If your vendor is not prepared to allow you to take the time you need to make your decision carefully, I would recommend you look elsewhere. When I have people come to choose a puppy, I am more than happy for them to take as long as they like. I have nothing to hide, and provided the pups are handled gently and with respect, I am more than happy to accommodate them. I would go as far as to say I prefer those people – it gives me confidence in their intentions as buyers. If, as often happens, the vendor keeps trying to steer you away from any particular pup, take no notice of his comments and make your own assessment; this may well be a pup that if he got stuck with one, this would be his preferred choice, so take no notice either in favour or against this pup and continue to carry out your own careful appraisal.

Whilst you have been examining the pups, the vendor will have no doubt been telling you all about the outstanding prowess of the puppies' parents. I wouldn't take any notice of that at all. It cannot be substantiated, and because of that do not allow it to cloud your judgement. You are trapped and forced to listen to it, but don't be influenced by it; an experienced person will very quickly be able to determine whether the seller is the real deal or a pretender, but someone looking for their first pup without any previous experience to help them should not be swayed by talk. Look at what is in front of you and do what you think is right for you.

We have now done all that we sensibly can in trying to secure the right pup.

Rumour at eight weeks, ticking all the boxes for me

On deciding to make the purchase, find out exactly how often and on what your pup has been fed. Most breeders will give you perhaps a week's supply that can either be mixed into the feed that you have decided to use or will last until you acquire more of the same. Puppy food will have a recommended rate and frequency of feeding on the bag, but do remember it is in the manufacturer's interest for you to feed your pup on their product longer than you need to. My pups at three months old will start to share the adult diet, and if you trial a bowl of puppy food next to a bowl of adult food at three months old, see which they prefer. Tread carefully, but don't be afraid of making your own decisions; should things not work, adjust, revert or change. Constant daily monitoring of your pup will give you all the information that you need.

Having done this, we have now selected our pup, which is by far the most important decision we will make. It is now completely up to us whether or not it makes the grade and reaches its full potential. If it does, it will be such a lovely feeling to be out alone at night with a dog you have trained, entered and are now working with together as a tight unit. If it doesn't, you will really need to take a hard look at yourself, because it will almost be a certainty that it will not be the dog's fault.

We have chosen our pup – it will now need a name. The dog won't care less what it is called, to him/her it is just a sound, so call it what you will; the easier to say its name the better, from my point of view – short names such as Tess or Moss, of which I have had many, have always been favourites of mine ahead of more regal-sounding titles carrying double or even treble syllables. The far more important factor at this point is that we have done everything we possibly can to secure the right pup, and in doing so our chances of success have significantly improved.

DIARY OF A LITTER (2)

When the pups were born there were just four – two black bitches and two dogs, one black and one brindle, all nice and healthy – and initially it appeared also very uniform in size which, was the first concern, as it was the smaller ones that would be of particular interest to me.

Dreaming of long windy nights ahead

Immediately on birth, it was also apparent that all the pups had inherited the lovely long back of their mother, a feature that I was particularly pleased to see and one which had played a large part in considerations when trying to select the right pairing.

At two weeks old, for worming purposes the first weighing took place, and it appeared that all four were doing well, but it also suggested that all four were heavier than what had been expected at this relatively early stage.

By four weeks old (2nd worming), whilst the pups were still of similar size to each other, there was, of course, a biggest and a smallest, although all still retained their noticeably longer than normal backs and also appeared to have noticeably longer than normal tails.

By four and a half weeks, the smallest – a black bitch – looked very tidy and appeared to have exceptionally nice feet, and for those physical reasons she had already started to catch my eye. However, it had also been noticed that whilst none of the pups were slow in coming forward, she was perhaps the most reserved; something that, of course, can be worked on, but I still like to take notice and register these early natural traits. Her brindle brother appeared the most confident and had to be first at everything; he was the smaller of the two dogs and because of this the black dog was not expected to become the final choice. An open mind – as hard as that is – must be kept until they are eight weeks old; at that time a decision on which to retain will have to be made. It is nice to see how frustrated the brindle dog gets when his larger sibling brother can climb out of their whelping box and he can't – point noted, and for me a natural indicator of his favourably developing character.

Five weeks old, the pups are now very mobile, eating as if there is no tomorrow, and now a real assessment can begin.

They all have nice feet and they all have long backs; these are typically early features that I habitually look for, but it doesn't help to narrow the choice when they all share the same positive attributes. The little black bitch is always the last out, the brindle dog always first; the black dog remains the biggest, but the second black bitch is looking really nice now she has inherited a white trim, perhaps from her distant Collie ancestor. She is possibly bigger at this stage than I would have ideally wished for, but nevertheless, her excellent conformation cannot be ignored as it starts to develop. Temperament-wise, she is not as forward as the brindle – none are – but she is certainly not shy. At this stage, if I had to choose, and fortunately I don't, I think it could easily be her. We will see what the next three weeks brings.

Six weeks old, and due to particularly bad weather, the pups have been coming indoors for their important socialising periods. This has been interesting and has presented an ideal time to really look at them closely, which in truth has not cleared the muddy water and made any firm decision forthcoming.

The smallest, the black bitch, was unsurprisingly the most put out by being in a new environment, but that quite quickly changed and she certainly has an edge and will not be bullied; you cannot help but like her.

The second black bitch with the white trim, very slightly bigger than her darker sister, showed no concern when confronted by a new environment. She seems to be a lot more even-tempered, confident and happy to go with the flow; her whole manner suggests that she would be very easy to train.

The brindle dog is the most affectionate of the four; he clearly loves human company and loves to carry anything he finds, which could have obvious benefits later. This is not really a trait that you would necessarily associate with a Lurcher pup of this breeding, but is very welcome nevertheless. He is a very nice pup.

The black dog is a real beauty, very handsome; he holds himself well even at this young age, and if you were going to pick a dog for showing or looks alone, he would definitely be the one; but because of his size and the fact that none of the other three have any currently identified defects that would rule them out of contention, he remains unlikely to become the final choice, as they all look like they could be a little bigger than what was hoped for, and of the group he is the biggest.

Still an open mind, but if I was choosing today it would be the brindle dog first and the bitch with white trim second.

Six and a half weeks old, the pups will continue to be monitored, but I think a decision has already been reached: two will be retained to start with and reduced to one at a later date. The two selected at present are the brindle dog and the black bitch with white trim. The black dog is probably the best overall specimen of the four, but is also now by quite a distance the biggest, and as size is important particularly with this litter and as all the pups appear bigger than expected, with his siblings being of a really pleasing standard, I am inclined to let him go.

Anybody who wanted a dog to show would snap him up straightaway; he is a real beauty.

The smallest black bitch which, out of the four, currently appears nearest to the size hoped for, is perhaps the lesser of the four in regards to overall quality, and there is perhaps a suspicion that her temperament may not be exactly how you would want it to be; so, despite her being marginally the smallest, it is the identified two that are the stand-out candidates, with the brindle dog, despite his antics at this moment in time, being the one that gives you that feeling of confidence that you can't explain, but he just feels right.

Seven weeks old, pups are now micro-chipped and have been photographed.

Eight weeks old, and the final choice has indeed been decided upon: the brindle dog and the bitch with the white trim are to be retained. Both look just as you would like them to, other than perhaps their current marginally larger than expected size. Neither has a defect that can be seen at this moment in time. The brindle, being the slightly smaller of the two, is currently the most likely at this stage to become the final choice. Both will receive basic training and we will make sure that whichever leaves us at a later date will be an excellent pup for someone to finish off and have ready for winter 2021.

Eight weeks old, the two unselected pups leave for their new homes. The two retained pups have been booked in at the vet's for their inoculations, and both have started to retrieve a rolled-up pair of socks indoors – only a couple of throws each at a time, but both like to chase and both are more than happy to return with their catch!

Training proper will start when they are inoculated and able to venture out into the world beyond the garden gate.

CHAPTER 4
TRAINING

For some people, the training process of their new Lurcher puppy is a chore. Why these people even take up our sport I cannot imagine, but presumably whatever the reasons are, they are surely not the right ones. As with so much in life, the more effort you are prepared to put in to this, the training stage of your pup, the more you can hope to be rewarded later.

Having been so careful in the selection of our puppy, to not apply the necessary effort at this really formative, crucial and yet also very enjoyable stage would be unforgivable. If you need persuading that this is so, perhaps you may like to ask yourself whether you would like to eventually be able to go out for a night's sport with a dog that you will barely need to talk to, who is an absolute joy to be with, who does absolutely everything you want it to do in a manner you would choose for it to do, or would you perhaps prefer to go out with a dog who, through absolutely no fault of its own, is a complete nightmare, cannot even be trusted to return to the handler, or ruins all chances of success by its general misbehaviour due to its owner's neglect at this training stage, so that consequently the dog has no realistic chance of ever fulfilling whatever natural potential it may have been born with.

Over the years, I have been out for various reasons with many other lampers, and on occasions absolutely despaired at some of the antics that I have witnessed from both the so-called lampers and their dogs – dogs that failed to return to their handler, dogs that could not be trusted to enter a field and wait for the handler without disappearing into the darkness, dogs that wouldn't even walk sensibly on the lead, in some cases to the point of practically strangling themselves. One particularly bad example of this, where the dog's handler (I don't even want to call him a lamper) had actually convinced himself that this totally unacceptable behaviour was derived through the dog's keenness and was actually a positive which he felt deserved to be commended! I rest my case.

A well-trained dog is the only thing that should interest us at this stage, and being prepared to put in the relatively modest necessary effort to achieve this goal is no hardship for us.

The training of any kind of working Lurcher is really no more than a slight extension of the basic training that any breed of dog should and deserves to receive. Our dogs, unlike many other working breeds of dog, cannot depend on us to constantly tell them what to do and when to do it. Whilst they are working they have to work a lot of it out for themselves; our job is to prepare them so that when certain predictable moments occur during the night, they know exactly how to deal with them and what to do.

From the moment we leave home to the moment we slip the dog on the first rabbit of the night, the dog should behave within the guidelines of what we have taught it. On the conclusion of that run, whether that particular rabbit has been caught or missed again, the dog must behave and react in the way it has been trained to do. Between these two moments, what is essentially the most important part of any night, the dog is on its own, and we become the passenger, spectator, totally reliant on our canine partner to keep the night going in the direction we want it to go. Our dogs – unlike certain other breeds – are not blessed with any kind of super-intelligence, despite what your pub lamper may have tried to convince you. But what they do have, however, is more than enough intelligence to satisfy our needs, and they are quite easily trainable to a standard where they will be able to efficiently carry out all of the tasks that we require them to do for us.

We should expect rabbit lamping puppies to be ready to enter by ten months of age. I say *should*, because there is no fixed rule; each pup is individual and it is important that we remember this and make sure that they are completely ready both physically and mentally before they start work. I would always opt to delay entering a pup if I thought it wasn't quite ready; many pups have been spoilt or at least detrimentally affected by starting too young – there is no rush. So, from a training point of view, we have approximately eight months from now to get our pup to where we want it to be. Time is definitely on our side, and because of this favourable situation, many owners succumb to the temptation of delaying the training process, which invariably gets put off and put off and then eventually never happens, or at best gets squeezed into a much shorter period of time than is really required, and as a result none of the lessons covered are properly digested and ingrained. Any problems that may be and almost certainly will be encountered along the way are not afforded the appropriate attention, and before you know it your pup is ready to start and you take a chance on leap-frogging training all together, wrongly believing that you will catch up as you go along, and things will then very quickly deteriorate and go steadily from bad to worse.

If you are serious about trying to do the best you can and in return expect to get the best out of your pup, work out a sensible schedule with a definite idea of where you want to be at what age, working within a timeframe that you know with certainty that you can dedicate to your pup – fifteen minutes a day on average is more than enough if time is spent wisely to get to where you need to be. Starting is the hardest bit; once you have, and you begin to see encouraging progress, it becomes so much easier and enjoyable to keep up the effort.

A word of warning here: do not over-extend your training sessions. A little and often is the remedy for success, and always try to leave each session on a positive note; and if for any reason you are in a bad mood on any particular day, don't even attempt training your pup. If your bad mood coincides with things not going well during your training session and you over-react unnecessarily, you will take a giant step backwards. Far better to miss a day's training than ever risk the possibility of that happening; your dog's state of mind and the relationship between you and your dog is everything.

Whether we have bought the pup in or have bred it ourselves and its litter mates have now departed, at approximately eight weeks old, for the first time in its short life, the pup is on its own. Now is a good time to spend as much time as possible with him/her, and in doing so become the new focus of its attention. A name will have almost certainly been decided upon, and this is a good time to teach it what it is called. A successful response to the call of its name can be rewarded with a tasty morsel. The name will become a sound that the puppy will very quickly learn to respond to by returning to you when hearing it, albeit initially for all the wrong reasons, but that matters not; as the response gets better, treats can be alternated with praise, which, as your relationship grows, will be deemed an even better reward than a treat, and eventually just the occasional treat will suffice – we all like them! Early attempts at the recall should take place in familiar surroundings without all the distractions that a new, unexplored area will provide. To make the lesson easier, restrict using the pup's name initially for moments where you can already see that the puppy is clearly certain to be coming your way. Cheating? Perhaps, but who cares? This is the easiest way to succeed; calling its name when the pup's attention is elsewhere or its intentions are clearly focussed on other things is never going to bring the positive outcome we are looking for at this early stage. Later, of course, you will be entitled to expect to be able to call its name at any given moment, no matter what else may be occurring, and yet still expect a favourable response – but that is for later. Today, if we need to cheat to tip everything to our favour, then cheat we will.

During these early informal sessions, as with all other training sessions that follow, it must be remembered that initially we are asking and showing the puppy what we want it to do. We have to be understanding and allow for individual specimen differences. They are all different; some find one thing difficult to grasp and something else seemingly easy, while other puppies could quite easily be the reverse. On our part, we have to try hard to put the pup more often than not in a position where it is bound to succeed; this way, genuine progress can be made and, most important of all, with the puppy's self-esteem firmly intact. Later, when we are absolutely certain that any lesson is completely understood, we no longer ask them to do something – we *tell* them, and we expect it to happen. If it does not, we must enforce our wish on the pup and make sure that it understands who is in charge. Every time that this happens, though, we must show the pup we will not tolerate disobedience, but equally we must recognise that we are usually to blame for these slight failings. If taught properly, deliberate disobedience should be a very rare occurrence; perhaps more confident pups needing slightly more correction than their more quiet-natured counterparts.

Nothing about the future working capabilities of any individual pup can be read into these different natural characteristics that the pups possess and reveal at this time. I have had really well-behaved, quiet scholars who grew into dogs that literally couldn't wait to get into the van to go lamping at night; precisely the attitude we are looking for. Other, seemingly more stronger-character pups during training, which did not show the same amount of enthusiasm when it came to their work, had you gone by their puppyhood temperaments this would almost certainly be a reversal of what you may have predicted.

All, however, must appreciate who is the boss. If verbal punishment is not sufficient, in extreme cases of undoubted disobedience I hold the pup firmly under the chin and growl at it. Nothing beyond that has any merit, and nothing beyond that is ever necessary. This type of punishment is reserved for later, older pups only; by the time you get to this age, the pup will have grown to appreciate your praise so much that just being told off will come as such a massive blow to its feelings that it will be extremely reluctant to repeat the same crime in the future. Consistency is key from both sides – you must always initially ask and show, later always tell, and the pup must always obey, always first time and, most importantly, always must mean *always*.

By the time the pup is ten weeks old and inoculated, it will now be eligible to go for walks beyond the confines of the garden. Before this can take place, it will need to be familiar with a collar and lead – no puppy is ever going to like that trade-off, and with the frustrating absence of being able to explain what is happening, we have to go through the process and help them get used to this unwanted restriction.

Lead training

Nothing seems to faze Rumour

Right at the beginning of the training stage I would like to point out that I never walk my lamping pups where they may see or especially smell a rabbit; there is absolutely nothing to be gained from it, but the pups may be encouraged to start following their noses, having made contact with this alluring scent. Later, when they are working at night, literally the last thing we want them to do is to start using their noses, so I do nothing to encourage it, even at this tender age.

The collar should be very light and can start being put on at about eight/nine weeks for short periods only; initially, if the pup is home-bred I would not recommend the use of collars until all the other siblings have gone – it will only get ruined and be used to potentially drag weaker siblings around, so I prefer to wait. It will cause irritation at first and the pup will rub and scratch in intermittent attempts at removing it, eventually accepting it after a few days.

The lead proves much more restrictive and as such is disliked even further. I find the best way to introduce the lead is to sit down with the puppy, clip on the lead but remain stationary and try to pass this introductory phase as conflict-free as possible by offering a reward, indulging in a game and generally doing anything that prevents the lead pulling tight, then periodically taking it off and putting it back on. Certain puppies will be more determined than others with regard to their efforts not to conform and accept, but all eventually will. When it comes to actually going for a walk, distance covered during these early lessons are completely immaterial. Ten yards, one hundred yards, it matters not – the important factor is getting the pup to tolerate this new and unwanted restriction. Some will accept almost immediately, some take longer; gentle handling is an absolute requirement with all.

First experiences with traffic can be traumatic, so time your walk to coincide with the prospect of as little traffic as possible, preferably none at all to start with. I always pick my pup up should a vehicle approach; this allows me to monitor any reaction with the pup safely in my arms. Later, when I feel that they are ready, I leave them standing on the ground and bend down to them as the vehicle passes, constantly reassuring them. If all is going well or when this stage is reached and passed satisfactorily, the same exercises are repeated in the dark. Common sense and careful, considerate handling can certainly influence the time it takes before the puppy is trotting comfortably along beside you in any location at any time of day. Up until this point has been reached, I will happily accept a puppy pulling forwards on the lead, but from this point on I gradually educate them that pulling is no longer going to be tolerated. People training their first running dog will notice that a leaf blowing in the wind, a blackbird hopping down the path in front of you, will all need chasing; this is a perfectly normal behavioural trait, and the sighthound instincts are starting to reveal themselves.

When lead training has been successfully mastered, the way is now opened for other important basic lessons to be considered. These may now be taught whilst at times, if necessary, retaining the pup under close control. On reaching this stage, you may also have become really encouraged by your apparent success and delighting in the response you are receiving from your pup. That is great and a perfect start has been made, but just as postponing training should never happen, nor should overdoing it. Never let the pup become bored with restrictions; basically, let the pup be a pup. Just as a child at school has a playtime, so should our pups; just make sure that nothing that it does whilst playing contradicts the good you have so far achieved. Be sure that anyone else, particularly family members, for example, who come into contact with your pup, know clearly what are and are not acceptable games to play. The most obvious of these is retrieving, but that is a definite no to anybody else but the trainer. Should the pup deliver something to them naturally, which rarely happens at this stage with our breed, you could tell them how you would like them to respond, praise, of course, being essential – but under no circumstances allow anybody other than yourself to instigate the exercise.

So we now have a pup gaining in confidence, walking on the lead and generally loving life. The remaining disciplines that we need to cover and fully master before the pup reaches ten months old include Sitting, Lie Down, Stay, Walking to Heel, Retrieving and Jumping. After years of trying various ways, I am now perfectly settled and happy to recommend dividing this group of lessons into two. The first four on our list are all things that we can comfortably teach our pup, but none of which it will particularly enjoy. The commands will be obeyed because we have taught the pup that they must be, but that doesn't mean our pup enjoys it. The last two – retrieving and jumping – they love. If covered properly and made enjoyable, as they should be, these two lessons are never a chore.

So I would say one from each group can comfortably be taught simultaneously, never moving on to the next until we are certain that the current lessons are completely understood, the command being at all times immediately obeyed. I don't think it really matters in which way you approach the first group, but if we go Sit, Lie, Stay, one lesson follows on nicely from its predecessor; in group two, if we cover Retrieving first and then move on to Jumping, when we feel ready we can quite easily combine the two as we progress and feel ready for the next discipline. Every two or three training sessions I would have a refresher of what has already been taught, so that it really becomes ingrained and never gets forgotten. In addition to these "refresher" sessions, there will be a lot of opportunities to revise what has already been covered in training during normal daily exercise/play activities, none of which should be missed, but equally none of which should ever be overdone.

Next we move on to Sit, probably the simplest lesson of all. For sensible, quieter puppies it can easily be attempted free from the restraint of the lead; for more headstrong pups who habitually find it harder to pay attention, it may be better initially if they are aware that they are on the lead, as this may well help proceedings run smoother. The trainer will decide what is best for the particular pup with which he is working.

Whatever has been decided, find a nice quiet location free from distraction and with the puppy beside you, command 'Sit', whilst at the same time, with one hand on their chest and one on their rump, manoeuvre them into the sit position. Some pups literally only need this to be carried out three or four times before it is understood and carried out on command. Others – I guess it is fair to say the majority – take longer, but all get the hang of what is required very easily. Praise at this age can never be overdone, and each time the pup successfully carries out any instruction praise should be offered in abundance and way over what the accomplishment really warrants.

Pups who need more than just a few lessons of learning the command 'Sit' will invariably succumb to bribery – the lesson suddenly becomes much easier to understand when it is supported by reward. This is fine. Some pups need this, some don't, but all are revealing their personality traits, which will help us in deciding how to progress through the other perhaps more difficult stages. Those that are inclined to need bribery should not be overly rewarded once they have proved to us that they understand a command, but the knowledge that this is how their mindset works helps us to use this information to our own benefit when working with them. The more sensible, mature-type puppies can also be rewarded on successfully carrying out any instruction; this just reinforces the message that you are pleased with them and for some (the easy ones) this is all they want.

Sit

As 'Sit' becomes understood, you, of course, no longer need to put them into the position, so with your hands now free, the 'Sit' command can be accompanied by the raising of a hand, palm facing the puppy. If you persist with this verbal and hand combined instruction, your dog will gradually, through repetition, associate your hand alone as the command to sit. The length of time that this takes is totally unimportant, but providing you are consistent and ensure that you make the signal always well within the dog's level of understanding, the penny will eventually drop and you have a dog sitting to hand signal only. 'Sit' command now digested, instruct them to do it, offer praise, walk on slightly, then instruct 'Sit' again; this will reveal that the sound/word is completely understood. Some pups may crouch as if to sit, but not actually complete the movement. Do not tolerate this. 'Sit' means sit every time, without exception. If necessary, growl at them, then once again use your hands to put them into position, but this time with no praise. The next 'Sit' will almost certainly be carried out in a much more appropriate fashion and due to this, praise can and importantly must immediately be given. You are learning about the personality of your pup and they are learning about yours. What we want them to understand about us is that when we give a command we expect it to be immediately carried out; we are not going to accept anything less, but when it is carried out immediately and satisfactorily, we will be very appreciative and a much easier person to get along with.

'Lie Down' follows 'Sit'. It is a simple extension to 'Sit' that some pups actually show a natural preference for – they take up this lying down position very readily, particularly when the 'Stay' lesson has commenced. Nevertheless, as we know, time is on our side, so we persevere with our lessons and educate the pups to the two distinctly different instructions. If your pup needs encouragement – and most will – whilst they are in the 'Sit' position, extend their front legs whilst applying pressure to the shoulder area, push gently down and give the command to 'Lie Down'. I tend to just use 'Down', but you can say whatever you want; however, make it simple and be consistent. When you have your pup that without any fuss at all you can get to sit, then lie, then move back up to the sit on command without moving from the very spot it initially occupied at the beginning of the exercise, you are well on your way and your puppy is doing just fine.

Lie [down]

These two lessons, it could be argued, have no beneficial impact on training a Specialist Rabbit Lamping Lurcher. It is true that the number of times these instructions will ever be given during a night's lamping are probably non-existent; however, I would always recommend that the basic lessons are taught, as it is quite likely that in its lifetime there will be occasions when your dog accompanies you ferreting, and these lessons on those days will prove invaluable. Perhaps more importantly for us at this particular time, in trying to create our perfect specialist lamping partner we are establishing roles and instilling discipline. These early simple lessons offer either directly or indirectly much to gain with absolutely nothing to lose, so I would always strongly recommend the training of both.

"Stay" here is a command that I feel betrays a lot of the natural personality and disposition of your pup. Some – the sensible, mature, steady ones – are more than happy to stay, to sit down, and watch suits them just fine; others – perhaps more mischievous and of stronger dispositions – struggle terribly to bring themselves to obey this boring command which goes completely against their grain. You will probably be able to predict with a reasonable level of accuracy from quite a young age which pups will and which pups won't struggle with staying. As with all the lessons we teach them, all dogs, of course, will eventually conform.

Again, we must not read too much into the manner in which our pups respond to this singular but much more important command; however, I have to say that personally the best two lamping dogs – or in their case, bitches – I have ever had – one of which to this day was the best Rabbit Lamper I have ever seen – were both far harder than any pup should be to train to stay.

'Stay' is easy enough, or at least should be; the awkward ones just take longer, as you need to go slower with them. There is absolutely no difference in what you do, other than the distance, and time is in much smaller segments and so, of course, to get to the stage you want to accomplish with this lesson takes much longer. Time we know we have plenty of, and this lesson more than any other is, in my opinion, crucial. You could compile a list as long as you like as to when this command is likely to be used or needed whilst the dog is working; however, the importance of it is such that ultimately, in extreme circumstances, it could even save the dog's life, so although I would strongly recommend the basic standard of 'Sit' and 'Lie', the 'Stay' is an absolute must.

With our pup in the sit or lie (down) position, simply raise your hand as before, only this time with your elbow bent, as you command 'Stay' in a slow, drawn-out manner, then extend your arm, bringing the palm of your hand close to the dog's face, repeat 'Stay', take one backward step, which will suffice to start with, then return to your pup and praise it, although having achieved so little it will probably wonder what the fuss is about. This matters not – when the command has been associated with remaining still by your pup, the distance that you may move back away from the pup will extend by ever-increasing margins. The first five yards are the hardest; by then the pup will have grasped the idea and then, providing you don't try to go too fast, you are winning. I used to make a pup stay and after a certain but ever-increasing amount of time waiting, then call the pup to me. I now realise the error of this method and now, when you have either moved away to the intended distance or waited for the appropriate time, I strongly recommend that you return to your pup and resist the temptation of calling it to you.

Being taught by this method, the pup will find it much easier to understand that 'Stay' really does mean stay. My previous flawed method does nothing but build anxiety in the waiting pup; so desperate is it to hear you call it to you, the longer the delay, the higher the level of expectancy will build, until eventually the pup is overcome with anticipation and spoils the moment by moving and creeping or even running in. So now, having learnt the error of my ways, I would recommend, following the 'Stay'

Stay [wait]

command, you move away as far as you think appropriate for as long as you consider necessary, based purely on the pup's particular capabilities at that particular time, always being sure to never over-extend what you try to achieve, whilst gradually increasing to perhaps a hundred yards, then waiting for perhaps a full five minutes before you return. When the puppy is successfully staying at this distance for that amount of time, you can be confident that the lesson is fully comprehended. Then, and only then, and to start with only very occasionally, you may choose to mix it up a little and on occasions call the pup to you from the staying position.

If at any time during the lesson of staying the pup moves, go to it and with your hand gripping under its chin, take it back to where it was originally stationed, over-emphasise the command 'Stay' and try again; this time do not overdo it, before returning and praising the pup, whilst remembering that the real reason for that slight mishap was almost certainly the result of you trying to be too clever or too quick and the blame really lies with the trainer, not the pup. Nevertheless, as always, remain consistent – 'Stay' means stay.

Walking at heel for a puppy that is now already lead-trained is a formality. During your initial lead training, you reached the point where it was felt that any fear or resistance to the lead was a thing of the past: walking along highways, vehicles were ignored, and the puppy was trotting along with an air of confidence. This, as previously mentioned, is the moment when pulling on the lead changes from something we can temporarily live with to something which is most unacceptable. During the correction process of converting the puppy to walk nicely beside you as opposed to pulling in front, we can take the opportunity to also teach our pup to walk to heel.

'Heel', I appreciate, is the generically used command, but for a reason I no longer remember, I use the term 'Back'. As with all other lessons, it really doesn't matter what term you use, just as long as you are consistent with it. As you walk along, the puppy, as has become its way, starts to move ahead; use the lead to move it back beside you, whilst commanding 'Back'. Continue to repeat this monotonous exercise whilst carefully paying attention to the puppy's behavior – you are basically watching and waiting for an excuse to praise it. This moment may come quickly or it may take a while, but as soon as the opportunity to praise develops via good behavior, use it; often, our pups receive praise in the early stages of any new discipline and I am certain they don't even know the reason for it. That doesn't matter: they like it and eventually they will realise that when you say 'Back' and they walk beside you, they get praise; that is the precise moment in each stage of training where we start winning.

When you are certain that the puppy understands what 'Back' means, always continue to praise good behavior, obviously leaving longer gaps between these moments of praise. The more accomplished at whatever you are teaching the pup becomes, you must now also stop tolerating poor behavior. When you say 'Back', you mean back. Things will slot into place very quickly, and we now have a puppy walking at heel, at least whilst they are on the lead. When the puppy's response suggests we can move on, this lesson can then be continued free of the lead, providing all has gone well, extending both the duration of time and distance you travel before replacing the lead once again.

Again, repetition is our accomplice; always take your time, always pick the right places, always pick the right times, and always remain firm but fair.

Walking to heel [back]

Later, when we are out at night, there will be moments when we want our dog near us, but perhaps it is, for some reason, impractical to have it on the lead – walking along a narrow overgrown lane or cutting through woodland, for example – we want to be certain our dog is with us in the darkness without having to check, so we want to be able to give the command with confidence that it will be adhered to. By the time we have reached this more advanced stage, the dog will instinctively know what is going on and 'Back' can mean anywhere close behind, to the side, anywhere where it can pick its own path without getting in front and, worse, still trod on, and yet still remaining close by.

Retrieving for a Rabbit Lamping Lurcher is an absolute must – there is absolutely no argument that could ever be had that this is not so. There is no point even considering an alternative – there isn't one. Our dogs must retrieve.

Not only must they retrieve, they must do it gently and they must do it fast. If they don't do it gently with live rabbits brought carefully back to hand, then the carcasses are going to be damaged, perhaps even to the point of being unsellable, which will completely defeat our purpose.

Rabbits are gregarious creatures. They are most likely to be found in the company and close proximity to others of their own kind, and if our dogs don't pick up the rabbits they catch and bring them back immediately, it is going to detrimentally affect the number of further opportunities available to us from any individual field. Because of this failing, it will, in due course, inevitably lower the night's bag. Rabbits are not just going to sit there for us, waiting to be caught; as with a lot of heavily preyed-upon creatures, rabbits may not be particularly intelligent, but they know what they need to know and have been gifted with a very acute sense of danger – when they sense danger, they don't ask questions, they act on it, so when we make contact with a group of feeding rabbits, we need to act as fast as we efficiently can. A dog that mucks about with its catch is not at all what we want. This type of dog is one that on any particular night is going to significantly affect the numbers caught; multiply that by the number of times you go out with it in a season and now you will certainly be entitled to be concerned. The standard that we strive for would be: just as soon as the rabbit is picked up, the dog's immediate thought and subsequent action is to come straight back and return to hand with its catch. There is nothing a rabbit lamper enjoys more than seeing a dog pick up a rabbit and turn to retrieve without breaking stride or have any notable reduction in speed. This is the elite standard that we must aim for at all times with our dogs.

Fortunately for us, despite not being a natural retrieving breed, retrieving is a discipline that our dogs can easily be taught. Done correctly, it starts as a game they love to play and, unlike the boring sit, lie and stay, becomes an exercise they will look forward to.

Most puppies will find something to play with; it may be something that you have provided, it could be just a stick or an old bone. Providing it is not oversized or too heavy, it will do nicely for us to start with. Get down on the ground with the pup and share the excitement of whatever it is that is clearly holding their attention. The pup is now beside itself, as not only does it have its chosen toy, but it also has you. Life at that precise moment could not get better than this! Hold the item and perhaps tease a little; when the pup is completely focussed on whatever it is it has been playing with, just toss it maybe a yard away. Make sure the pup can always see it, so not in long grass or anywhere that it could possibly go out of sight. Instinctively, the pup will chase it, and as it is already something that the pup is very familiar with, it will not hesitate to pick it up. At that precise moment, squeak, call, do whatever you need to do to get the pup to come back to you. This should be straightforward, and its first retrieve has been completed. The fuss you make will not register as a direct reaction to what it has just done, but nevertheless, the pup will be happy to repeat the process as it is fun all the way. Having completed a repeat performance, stop. That's it – the game is over. Make a big fuss of the pup, but nothing can be gained from continuing. Should the fickle attention of your pup decide that a new game is needed, a failure to bring back the toy would be a massive step backwards. Better to quit while we are ahead – tomorrow we play the game again, after being careful to observe what the toy of the day is, as it may well be different to yesterday's. If there is no toy of the day, we can start to provide one: a glove, a rolled-up sock, a rag tied into a knot; anything like that will do nicely. Always make sure that whatever you play with can easily be seen where it lands. There is a very good reason for this, as we only want to encourage the use of sight from our pup for as long as we possibly can – we don't want to encourage our dogs to hunt by scent. Later, when they are working at night, when a rabbit is missed they must return immediately to us to prepare for the next run. We certainly don't want them to start scent-hunting and disturb the whole field, so the last thing we want to do now is encourage it. So, making sure that the toy can easily be seen, throw it, allow it to be retrieved and make a fuss, in that order, always stopping when the game is at its peak. What is thrown can gradually be changed to something more fit for purpose, never allowing the object to be too heavy to be gently carried; imagine yourself picking up a brick, how much pressure you would need to exert in comparison to picking up a block – so it is with our pups: keep the object light.

Always play the game on ground that has been thoroughly investigated by your pup so that there is no likelihood of its attention being distracted. At home, of course, you should be safe, but if you are out together in an unusual place, turn around and throw back onto ground you have already covered and know to be free from any distraction and that has already been fully explored. Always make sure the pup retrieves all the way back and delivers into your hand – near enough is not good enough. At night you will not want to have to put the light on to see where your dog is; you want the rabbit brought all the way back and put straight into your hand, so start that process now and the pup will never know any different. Each time I send a pup to retrieve, I hiss, a sound that will later be used to say that a rabbit has been spotted when we are lamping. Any word will do instead. 'Fetch' is the obvious word, but it doesn't really matter what you use; however, now is the right time to teach your pup that it means go and bring it back to hand; instilling this instruction now will make life much easier for yourself later.

Retrieving at speed

Retrieving various objects

In time, if the pup starts to muck about and perhaps, for example, begins to deviate from a straight line whilst retrieving, find a suitable lane or alley where the opportunity to develop this bad habit is immediately eradicated. Restore order without delay; if the retrieve is not being carried out fast enough for your liking, as the toy or dummy is picked up and the pup turns to come back, start moving directly away from it. This will bring immediate improvement and speed up the process to how we want it to be. Watch carefully over your shoulder as the retrieve concludes and be ready to make a fuss of this much-improved performance.

There are no real rules as to exactly what we do, and unfortunately there is an enormous list of little habits that can develop during the training process, some we can live with, some we cannot. Those we cannot we need to eradicate before they become established. Always try to be one step in front by being observant: if something is not going well or is in danger of deteriorating, do not cross your fingers and hope for the best – take the initiative and put it right by whatever means necessary. During any training lesson, always bear in mind what we are aiming towards and never do anything that may in no matter how small a way affect our target of perfection.

Retrieving the thrown object will gradually improve, and in keeping with the pup's growth, new dummies can be introduced and distances sent will be extended. Towards the end of retrieving training, we need to introduce our pup to fur. We can either dry a rabbit's skin and carefully cover the dummy – this works perfectly well – or what I tend to do now is to use a dead squirrel with its tail removed. I am fortunate that my employment provides an unlimited supply of fresh carcasses to use and I appreciate it may not be quite so easy for everyone to have a constant fresh supply like that, but I do like using the squirrels as they are just the right size and weight and have nice tight, short fur which I consider to be perfect for an early introduction. Should the option of using fresh squirrels not be realistic, a fur-covered dummy is perfectly adequate. At this stage you should find somewhere quiet to sit down, allow your pup to come to you and then produce the squirrel/ fur-covered dummy without any fuss. Treating the whole thing in a calm and gentle manner, you can be almost guaranteed that your pup will show no alarm, and the fact that you are holding it will give the pup any additional confidence should it be required. This is most unlikely to be needed, but there is no reason to take any chances. When you can see that the pup is comfortable with it, a short retrieving session can be conducted, as always exaggerating the praise and as always watching for any sign of a bad habit developing. Finally, all other objects are disposed of and we can introduce a dead rabbit. A half-grown one is ideal to start with, before being replaced

The sight we look forward to becoming accustomed to

by a full-grown one. This, for me, is one of the best moments in training as, for the first time, we get to see a sight that we look forward to so much and one that will become so familiar to us in the future.

Training our Lurchers to jump is a divisive subject within the ranks of Rabbit Lampers. Some argue that it encourages dogs to jump into the darkness without being able to see the dangers ahead. Many years ago, I listened to this sentiment and, I assume like others, became naturally concerned about the possibility of this happening to one of my dogs. This sentiment didn't last for long. When you are loaded up with rabbits and live in an area like I do where the knowledge of how to hang a gate properly is yet to arrive and bailer twine has replaced both hinge and clasp, the last thing you want to be doing is continually lifting your dog over gates all night. Out alone at night, this much-held belief concerning lamping dogs jumping occupied my thoughts, and more and more I questioned the truth behind the myth. I was becoming more familiar with running dog behaviour and had already personally witnessed injuries that had been caused by dogs jumping that were not equipped to carry out the discipline effectively, having never been encouraged or taught. I decided that I was not happy with the logic behind the argument, and from that point on proceeded to teach my dogs to jump. That was decades ago and I have never for one moment considered it to have been an error of judgement. Yes, I suppose a dog in the heat of the moment could do something like jumping into the darkness unsighted, but I have never had one do it – that, of course, doesn't mean it can't happen, but it must surely by now demonstrate how unlikely it is. Injuries from jumping can happen particularly on barbed-wire fences, but I have seen far more injuries sustained by dogs that can't jump but try than I have from dogs that can jump proficiently. Anyway, I have for over thirty-five years taught my lamping dogs to jump and will, without any doubt, continue to do so.

Jumping is something that our naturally athletic dogs find simple, and for me to see a dog return and clear a fence or five-bar gate whilst retrieving its catch is a sight to behold. Jump training can start at any age from three to six months; the age doesn't really matter, as you will be the one who governs how high they are expected to go, and at all times you must make sure that every jump is both well within the dog's capabilities and carries no risk of any structural damage to young growing joints.

Jumping can start at home; perhaps a pathway between kennel and the garden, or something like that, where a six-inch board can be positioned to prevent clear passage. Each time the pup crosses the board, command 'Up'. Soon, the three things – command, action, praise – will be put together and the puppy's willingness to carry out this simple instruction will increase. At the appropriate time, a second board can be added, and continue in this vein

Learning to jump at home

as jumping improves and as the puppy grows. In addition, a second, more formal jump can also be constructed simply in the garden when the height being cleared over the boards has perhaps reached that of a long net. Here, with our purpose-made jump, the same principle can be used, but I would recommend using rails and leaving gaps between them; this replicates a five-bar gate perfectly, and this new obstacle will undoubtedly be treated and dealt with by your pup in the same nonchalant manner as the boards.

As the capabilities of your pup increase, always be on the lookout whilst out on normal daily exercise walks for walls, fences or gates that are of a suitable height according to the level you are currently at, which you may also utilise to get your puppy confidently jumping any obstacle it is asked to, familiar or not. It really is that simple – just always remember the golden rule of only asking the dog to jump what you know it comfortably

Jumping well within her capabilities

can. Never, under any circumstances, ask it to jump something to see if it can – that would be irresponsible and could easily undo much good work and severely affect future progress. You will be able to see when you are able to increase heights by how much current levels are being cleared by.

A standard five-bar gate is approximately four foot six inches high, so if we use this as our target to be attained by the pup at ten months old, it can be seen just how gradual we can afford to go. There is no rush, but throughout this stage remain over-generous with praise.

During the jumping training stage we can, when we feel it appropriate, double-up the lessons to include retrieving and have our pup retrieving and jumping at the same time. I will never tire of these types of exercises and love to watch the pup in action. Remember to never throw something over the jump for your pup to retrieve that may land somewhere where it

Jumping and retrieving combined and being carried out with confidence

becomes unseen, and never drop your guard and allow that to happen, for the reasons already mentioned.

Jumping is never a chore to our dogs: they find it so easy. I currently have a trained one-year-old bitch who habitually jumps back and forth over the jump that was erected for her and her sister in the garden which has been left in place for further use when the two pups in "Diary of a Litter" are ready to utilise it. She delights in jumping back and forth, waiting for praise and feeling very pleased with herself. Were she human, you would say she was showing off, but that certainly doesn't seem to bother her. Though the specialist type of Lurcher we require is small in comparison to many other Lurchers intended for different purposes, jumping a five-bar gate or fence of similar height is simple for them. Providing they have had the opportunity to learn and hone their skills, they will find no problem attaining the standard we require.

Back in the late seventies/early eighties, very often at country fairs they used to organise high

22in Bearded Collie-cross trained by the author, who appears to have once had hair! Back in the early eighties clearing 8ft 4in

jump competitions for Lurchers. It was only a bit of fun, and you could quite informally enter if you felt inclined. During that time, I had a Bearded Collie-cross which stood at just twenty-two inches to the shoulder, but despite her size she would regularly clear eight foot-plus on such occasions when asked to, so it can be seen from this one example, even if it may be slightly extreme, that what we are asking our dogs to do is easily well within their capabilities.

One final jumping lesson that I consider to be well worth the effort of covering, one that undoubtedly will frequently become useful to have at your disposal, is to teach your dog to use your arm to jump over when the dog's safety is a concern. Very often during a night's lamping you may come across an awkward-angled fence with barbed-wire posing a significant threat of injury; it is quite simple to lay your arm along the top and have your dog use your arm as a rail, jumping over it and being shielded from the dangerous wire beneath. Now is the time to teach it. Find or even create a suitable location to start with, and a competent jumper that trusts its human companion will soon master this useful exercise.

Livestock training is an absolute must. You may find it difficult to obtain permission to lamp, and having done so the last thing you want to do is lose it again by means of this unforgivable crime. It will not take long or be difficult to teach your pups that sheep in particular, but livestock in general, are off the menu. As always, be fair, but perhaps now more than ever be forceful – it is not acceptable and they must and easily will learn it.

If you have a contact in the farming fraternity, he may well be willing to help by offering access to a ewe with a history of standing up to be counted on such occasions. Should she have a lamb, better still; if your pup needs convincing, she may well take care of this easier than you will.

When our puppy has successfully completed and learnt all of these lessons, it will be as best equipped to start work as we can help it become. Following this training period there is so much more the pup must learn, but this we cannot teach it; the remaining lessons will be learnt through experience, success and failure. Each dog will have their own little traits, and each will attain differing standards. We, as handlers, must be prepared to recognise them and adapt our technique to take full advantage of any strengths that our dogs may prove to have, whilst also adjusting to help overcome any weaknesses they show in order that together in time we may forge a successful partnership.

What we have done by conducting this training programme is ensured that our pup has a solid foundation: it is now fully prepared and ready to be entered. Through our efforts and with our continued help, we have presented it with the opportunity of becoming a genuine first-class Rabbit Lamper in the future.

DIARY OF A LITTER (3)

Training.

Both puppies have started their basic training with confidence and both have happy outgoing temperaments both like retrieving which was started at a very young age so is of no real surprise, Shamus the dog particularly enjoys this game he has always shown a pleasure in carrying objects around so for that to be coupled with a game that ultimately leads to praise life really doesn't get much better than that for him.

Rumour the bitch whilst equally happy to retrieve does it in a much more dignified manner resisting to act the idiot that her brother feels is necessary whilst carrying out the same task. In neither way do I see any positive or negative just a difference in their mannerisms both pleasing and perfectly acceptable in their own way . Rumour is currently more business like but Shamus will calm down in time of that I am quite certain.

Both showed no concerns with having their collars on, being homebred and completely trusting of us choosing the right time to put them on and take them off overcame that hurdle without any kind of incident. The addition of the lead to Rumour was not in anyway a problem and with gentle care she was soon trotting along very nicely, Shamus however did not consider the lead to be a step in the right direction and so put up mild resistance but was soon bribed into submission and eventually accepted that life did in fact apparently have restrictions and like his sister although perhaps not quite so quickly soon accepted the lead.

Sit for both was simplicity Rumour again responding more maturely than her brother but both very quickly learnt and obeyed the command to sit.

A final decision has been made and Rumour has become the puppy selected to proceed with she is everything that was hoped for when her parents were initially selected and despite early concerns about her size she is now actually looking like she may end up around about the right size, Shamus initially was the smaller of the two retained pups but has now quite noticeably over taken his sister. In many ways i have surprised myself by selecting Rumour because throughout although I tried to keep an open mind I think i subconsciously thought that Shamus would probably become my final choice, he, as nice a puppy as he undoubtedly is I think is going to be bigger than what is ideally required, in the absence of his Sister and her obvious quality's I would have been more than happy to have kept him but I have full confidence in Rumour she appears to be developing into everything I had hoped for from this litter and so intend to find Shamus a nice home and invest all my time and effort into her.

Rumour at four months old

Rumour

Shamus

Rumour at eight months old

Someone is going to be lucky and have a genuinely nice puppy in Shamus.

Rumours retrieving sessions although very much enjoyed have just started to deviate from how you would like it to be. She is four months old now and has started to run slightly wide of where I am standing on her return so I intend to start a spell of retrieving in narrow lanes to correct that before it develops into a habit.

One excusable cause for this deviation is the speed at which she travels back with either tennis ball or Dummy making it hard for her to instantly stop this is appreciated and understood but we need to work on correction before we try and move on any further, the retrieve must be fast which we have but also must be direct which we do not have, it would be far easier to ignore this slight problem and accept what we have but my preference would always be to put it right now while we can and engrain the right behaviour having done so I know I will be so grateful that I did many, many times in the future.

Sit is completely understood and is now obeyed with just a raised hand and so we have moved on and started the "lie" or in our case "down" command, for a reason that I was unable to identify Rumour initially appeared to associate the command "down" with being told off and although she fairly quickly learnt what was required she avoided eye contact in carrying out "down" she distinctly turned her head away whilst complying. I have no idea why that happened or what caused it but it must surely have been my fault however with the use of treats and praise she was quickly reassured and the lesson was learnt with our relationship still firmly in tact she is a joy to work with as her whole attitude lends itself to training but this episode proves how easily you can go wrong and how no matter how much experience you may think you have you never stop learning.

Stay was our next lesson which also proved to be no problem at all and very quickly Rumour when told to "stay" would lie down, her body language revealed with quite a degree of certainty that she had no intention of moving once told to stay, as pleasurable as this easy step proved to be I think you could have predicted this would be her reaction to this lesson from quite a young age she has her moments of course as all puppy's do but throughout she has invariably behaved in a very mature manner for her age.

The ease at which this lesson was accomplished did not pass without remembering how difficult the same stage has previously been with some of the other dogs that I have trained which later in their lives went on to become first class lampers I am quite sure that there is nothing to read into this but previous experiences allow comparison and that is one that I always think of at this stage in a perverse way almost hoping that puppies prove difficult to train to stay is a bizarre sentiment based on what is surely nothing more than a coincidence that I have had success in the past with dogs that were difficult to train in this discipline.

Anyway what ever the facts are Rumour was very easy to train to stay overall she is progressing well and what is of equal importance is that I am now becoming more and more confident that she is not going to be oversized as initially feared. She is currently six months old and just a little over 21” to the shoulder using a self constructed graph that I have formulated over the years with the other pups I have trained of similar breeding her current height is around about where it should be and is on

Rumour at six months old

the right trajectory to meet the 23" to the shoulder that was initially hoped for. I feel very fortunate about this as when the pups were smaller I felt fairly certain that they were all going to be bigger than what I had hoped for, I am delighted to have been mistaken.

Walking to heel or in our case "Back" has been encouraged for some time now whilst Rumour is on the lead and we have now progressed with this discipline having seen that the command is certainly understood we dispense with the lead at suitable times and continue with her walking to heel bare necked. This lesson has gone well and now that I am sure she understands what is expected we are gradually extending the distance that she is expected to maintain walking at heel, later when it is felt she is ready I will increase the difficulty by expecting her to continue walking to heel with obvious distractions that she must ignore. I have no doubts or reservations about that being a success due to her obvious willingness to please and provided as with the "Stay" lesson that I don't try to much too soon I can see we are not going to have any problems with these important lessons.

Jumping is the next lesson and has been started in the garden a simple rail between two posts that we both step over together proved in truth so easy to be a waste of time but never the less we start at the beginning. The next rail was added and then a third a couple of times Rumour decided that going around was easier than going over so a long net was run out across the garden and through the hurdle dividing the garden into two this made going around the jump impossible. This also proved revealing as she then showed a preference for jumping the net as opposed to the jump despite the net being quite noticeably higher. One interesting fact that came to light whilst taking photographs of her for this book was how far away from the jump she took off something that I hadn't picked up on in real time . Rumour enjoys jumping and uses her natural ability in this area often in our daily exercise periods, streams fallen trees anything she happens to encounter are invariably cleared without it seems any thought or effort being needed so teaching a dog to jump that can so clearly naturally jump was never going to prove difficult . Combining retrieving with jumping was simple and made the whole experience even better for her and excitement at the prospect of a jumping/retrieving session found her jumping back and forth the hurdle for fun whilst waiting for me to get dummies out of my bag this suggested I needed to up my game to keep up with her. We progressed to other less familiar obstacles away from home and her familiar surroundings without any noticeable interruption to progress and it is quite clear that jumping comes easy for her. We have not yet got to our target height of a five bar gate but current progress leaves no doubt that with careful progression that target will not prove either anything like beyond her capabilities or in fact very far away.

RUMOUR.

In many ways Rumour due to her willingness and mature character has not really proved to have been the best possible example to have used for this diary. She has been really simple and straight forward to teach and now has a perfect understanding of all she needs to know when eventually the time comes for her to be “Entered”. Before then we will continue to improve and extend some lessons Jumping, staying and walking to heel [Back] and continue revising others Sit, Lie [Down] and retrieving.

Not all puppy’s are as straight forward as she has proved to be but I hope that this diary may help when others perhaps need a comparison. The fact she has been so easy to train does not in any way mean she will excel at lamping Rabbits we will have to wait and see about that but what it does mean is that when her time comes she will at least know how to behave.

Many puppy's prove much more trying than she has been in getting to this stage but they will all conform providing you stay firm and fair.

Rumour is nine months old now and appears to have stopped growing the last three times she has been measured she has been the same height at just very slightly under 23" . At the conception of this litter she is exactly what I was hoping for and I am delighted with how she has turned out. Retrieving lessons are now often carried out with a dead rabbit replacing the dummy and she has learnt how to carry them in a nice balanced way, frequently jumping obstacles in doing so when the occasion demands.

Despite the puppy's being so uniform at birth the Black dog her biggest brother now stands at 27", Shamus has made 25" and her smaller sister 22" .This variation in size is far from unusual in litters of lurchers. Remembering that the Sire was 23" and the Dam 26" logic may have suggested that the pups would have been somewhere in between and yet at least 50%, you could even argue that 75%of the litter are not.

Born at the time of year that she was Rumour is unfortunately ready to enter at the wrong time of year [you cannot control when bitches come into season] and so she will be held back and entered in the Autumn when the ground has softened up and the harvest is in I am not at all worried by holding her back I have done exactly the same thing with many other dogs when necessary in the past including some which eventually developed into really good workers i have never detected any indication of harm having been done to them by such a delay.

We all like to think that our puppies are going to prove a bit special when their time comes , we can never be sure whether they are until it does, realistically I know that Rumour is unlikely to match many of the dogs that I have previously worked with purely because circumstances dictate that she wont get the chance to develop to that standard through absolutely no fault of her own. I am a dinosaur now and as a result my lamping trips are fewer, yet my enjoyment of being involved with Lurchers has never diminished resulting in my kennel being overstocked, the relatively modest workload I have for my dogs is now shared by a larger than required team but this hasn't in any way stopped me from enjoying the process of training Rumour to the highest standard that I possibly could and I am really looking forward to working with her when her time does eventually come.

CHAPTER 5
EQUIPMENT

Collar and Lead

There are a variety of options when it comes to choosing what collar and lead arrangement to use. If you visit a country fair, you will find stallholders with literally hundreds of differing styles, colours and made out of various materials. Some, no doubt, are good; some are, perhaps, okay; many are an absolute waste of money. Before you rush off and part with your hard-earnt money, consider what you do actually need.

I would say that the first essential thing that we need is a very lightweight collar and lead which we can use whilst training our pup to walk on the lead. A collar at this point is perfect in my mind because it prevents any kind of pressure squeezing on the puppy's neck, as a free-running slip lead would. Depending on how long it takes to get the pup walking nicely beside us at heel (back) will determine whether the initial collar is enough – it should be – or whether we need a second, bigger one to replace the first as the pup grows. As soon as my pups are walking nicely at heel, they never have a collar around their necks again: the collar and lead arrangement is replaced by a cord lead. These will have a ring that allows the noose to be made into the appropriate size with a stop that can be slid up the cord to keep the noose at whatever size you choose and a spliced handle arrangement at the other end. I wouldn't even bother considering anything else to use whilst out on normal daily exercise walks and outings. When the dog is off the lead, I pull the noose to the maximum and then put it over one arm and my head; this then sits nicely around one shoulder and is neither in the way nor has any chance of becoming lost.

At night, I always, without exception, run a dog off of a slip lead; this for me is the only way to keep everything organized, under control and to retain constant discipline. The dog grows to expect it and knows no other, and after probably trying most things over the years, I have not deviated from my current arrangement for a very long time.

Some people like to use a collar with a single strand belt or cord simply fed under one side of it and out the other so that when the time is right the belt/cord is released from one end and the dog is away. I do not like this method at all and would never want to run any rabbit specialist dog with a collar on. I want my dogs to plough into hedges if necessary to prevent an escaping rabbit, and I would not ask them to do that and then burden them with something that could easily get caught up and cause them to incur any injury.

There are specially made quick-release slip leads of varying designs that you can buy. They are quite costly, but certainly do what they are meant to do, normally by means of a small thumb press button arrangement on the side of a clever little pulley mechanism. I would never entertain one of those either. You can watch people at country fairs try them on their dogs for size and then, full of enthusiasm, walk off with this expensive ingenious device, believing they have made an excellent purchase. I know you can, because I have been one of those people. It was a long time ago now, but I was so keen to perfect my art that I was convinced this was the way forward. The slipping device is fine on the first run and perhaps for a short while after, but then gradually, as the night progresses and you are loaded up with more and more rabbits, it becomes increasingly hard to bend down in order to replace it on the dog's neck, if you haven't already lost it by then.

For as long as I can remember, I have used a simple piece of cord thick enough to be comfortable for the dog and strong enough to last. I tie a simple basic loop on one end and get that loop the size that literally just squeezes over my wrist. When I put that on at night it never comes back off, and is absolutely impossible to drop or lose as it is fixed on my arm for the night. Then, a second loop is formed down the cord; the important factor here is that the distance between the two loops is greater than the distance between your wrist and the dog's neck. The free end of the cord is then burnt and squeezed whilst melting to seal – this prevents any fraying. The burnt end of the cord can then be put around the dog's neck and through the second loop, thus creating a noose to restrain the dog, the free end is held and should the dog lunge for any reason, it will tighten, whilst the section of lead between the second loop and your wrist remains slack at all times, so all the pressure is held on the free end. At the appropriate time when we are ready to slip the dog, we release our grip on the free end and the dog is away, bare-necked and free from any additional risk of injury. We don't even have to think about the lead as it is impossible to drop because it is attached to our wrist, so we just concentrate purely on the job in hand. When the dog returns and we are ready to proceed, we simply once again feed the free end back through the second loop and then slip it over the dog's head and we are immediately ready to go again. No bending over – no matter how many rabbits we are carrying, our load stays on board and nicely balanced. This lead costs nothing at all and I would never consider changing from its use.

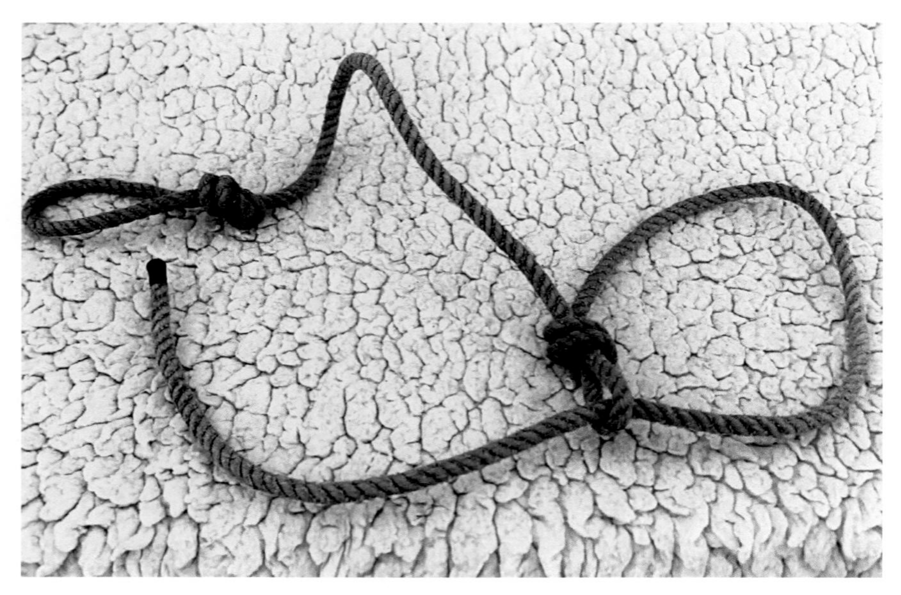

Simple but so effective slip lead

Lamp, Battery and Battery Charger

If we had a variety of options available to us with our leads, there appears to be a never-ending choice of lamps from which to choose. To the unknowing, it would seem fairly obvious that we would want the brightest light available; unfortunately, as nice as that would be, it would not suit our requirements at all. We do not want a lamp that is going to drain our battery too quickly and we do not want a lamp that is going to illuminate the countryside for miles around unnecessarily. What we ideally want is a nice, comfortable-to-hold, well-balanced lamp that provides us with a narrow beam with strength enough for what we are doing, but not so strong as to warn every rabbit in the neighbourhood of our impending visit.

My first lamp was a spotlight removed from a wrecked car in the local scrap yard that a friend took to work with him in the local dockyard, where he cleverly welded my spotlight onto a welder's torch handle. It had a dual-purpose trigger switch that you could either pull on or push up for permanent power. I thought it was great at the time, but looking back I now realise how cumbersome it was; but back then there was not a lot of choice that I was aware of and I spent several happy seasons using it, before recognising its weaknesses and searching for an upgrade. There is no need to use crazy fabricated things like that any more – at quite a realistic price we can obtain lamps which are absolutely perfectly suited to our needs.

The lamps most useful to us would be towards the bottom of the range available, as these days so much lamping is carried out using high-powered rifles, where the range and subsequent distance requirement is so much greater than ours. For us, a nice little lamp, perhaps six-inch diameter, clear glass fitted with a fifty-five-watt quartz halogen bulb, is perfect. Other considerations that may not spring to mind when choosing your model would perhaps include the switch: is it robust and quiet enough for our use? Also, the location of the switch: does it feel comfortable to hold up and switch on and off easily? Cable: is the cable coiled? This doesn't seem like a big deal but trust me, it is. My early lamps didn't have coiled cable and the amount of times I would catch the wires and pull them out was most frustrating, although at the time it was just accepted as an occupational hazard; of course, these days it doesn't need to be. Having mentioned these two factors to consider, if you do feel you have found the right lamp, you can always adapt it to suit your own need. Cables can soon be changed and if the switch appears weak or misplaced, modify or change it. For many years now I have used door-bell buttons for switches by removing the unwanted one, drilling out the casing and then screwing and finally taping the door-bell button into place exactly where I want it. It suits me fine, is simple to do, is easy and quiet to use and appears to last indefinitely. At each end of the cable I then create a further shock absorber by crimping back a slack length and taping it to the holding stem of the light, and doing a similar thing at the connector end using cord tied securely to a coil, and with this cord then attaching the cable to the battery box, leaving the created slack wire tucked

Ideal size and type of lamp, coiled cable taped to handle to provide additional protection against snagging and pulling cable out of light

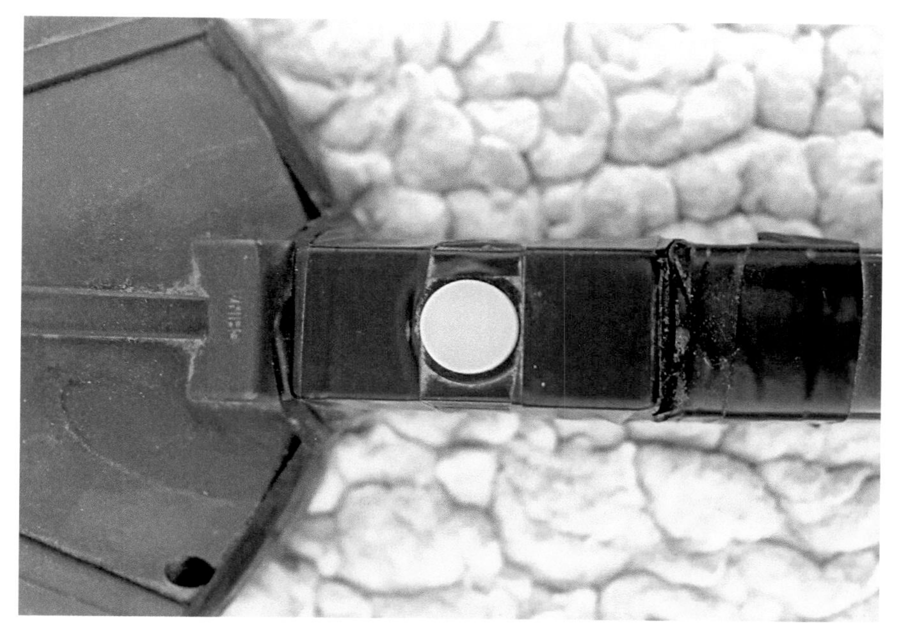

Door-bell on/off switch

into the box out of the way and with no pressure ever reaching the battery terminals. You will probably still occasionally catch and pull your wire out of your lamp, but much less frequently than had you not bothered to take these additional precautions.

A small lamp repair kit can be assembled and tucked away in the battery box for any on-the-hoof repairs should they be needed. Obviously we want to keep it to a minimum, but a small pair of pliers, some electrical tape and a small torch will all at some time prove useful.

Batteries have a much smaller selection from which to choose the one most suited to us. Happily gone are the days when you would wake up to find the acid spilt from the wet battery of old had burnt through your jacket, sometimes your trousers and on occasions even your underpants.

My choice of modern-day battery is a twelve-volt, seventeen amp hour dry cell model: it weighs approximately fourteen pounds and neatly fits into a purpose-built box with either a strong webbing or an old car safety belt carrying strap. Coupled with the right lamp and used sensibly, the battery gives a good lengthy session of usage before it begins to lose its power. A word of advice on the strapping of the box would be to take care when attaching it, and be sure to use two fixings on either end to ensure that the strap retains its flat surface and doesn't fold into a much narrower strip, thus concentrating all of the battery's weight onto a particular part of your shoulder, which will soon become uncomfortable. A nicely fitting battery

Purpose-made battery box, strong and wide webbing strap, industrial cable connectors compatible with either lamp, dependent on needs

box will nestle into the small of your back, and with a well-fitted strap spreading the weight you will hardly notice it is there.

I generally have three batteries in use at any one time and on leaving home for a night's lamping will often drop off and hide a fully charged replacement battery, if considered necessary, at a convenient place along my intended route. Both my batteries and my lamps are fitted with industrial-grade strength cable connectors, so when reaching one of these changeover locations, it is simple to untie the cable cord, pull apart the connector and swap batteries, leave the catch so far in a safe place hung up to cool and then continue with a full-strength battery empty-handed and ready to start again, returning to collect both the part-worn-out battery and the rabbits at the end of the night. A flask of tea is always a welcome addition to be left at these points, and never fails to hit the spot.

When it comes to charging the battery, I would recommend having an individual charger for each battery you use. As soon as I return home, the dogs get rubbed down, checked and fed first, then the rabbits get hung up, and then all batteries that have been used are immediately put on charge and left on overnight. A mechanic may well say that this is way over the top, but I don't care – this is what I do, and using this system I have always felt that I have received a good life duration out of each of the batteries that I have maintained in this fashion.

Carrying/Game Bag

With my battery box hanging on my right side from my left shoulder, I hang my game bag on my left side from my right shoulder. It is hung high enough that it cannot in any way aggravate or interfere with my dog, who habitually will be walking underneath it on my left-hand side.

I have carried out by far the vast majority of my lamping sessions single-handed, being unsociable; it is the way I have always preferred it. What this has meant is that I have usually had to carry everything I have caught; that is normally not a problem, but on certain successful nights, particularly those which coincide with very few possible drop-off points, it has certainly at times created its own challenge.

My usual system whilst lamping is that whilst working each individual field each rabbit caught is then placed into the game bag (which these days is exactly that, a specifically made bag for the job – years ago it was an old postman's bag which was made of a strong hessian, with the buckles taped up to stop them rattling! The younger generation will not remember these as I think postman's bags have been plastic and red for quite a while now). Anyway, each rabbit as it is caught goes into the bag, then, at the end of each field, just before vacating, the rabbits come out of the bag one at a time and get braced up on simple cord (bailer twine) strings. These strings are lengths of about twenty inches, with the two ends knotted together to form a loop. The loop is placed around the rabbit's two back legs just above the hock and then one end of it is pulled through the other, before being pulled tight to trap the rabbit's legs within. The other unoccupied end of the string is then pulled through itself to form a second noose, and the back legs of a second rabbit are placed in this before again being pulled tight.

This pair of rabbits are then placed over the right shoulder loops, being held shut by the weight of the rabbits. The process is then repeated, and if an odd number of rabbits has been caught in that particular field, the odd one will stay in the game bag into the next field, at the end of which the whole bracing-up process will be repeated. In a particularly good field it may be necessary to stop and brace-up before the field is finished, but this would be rare and I would always try and avoid it, unless your dog needs

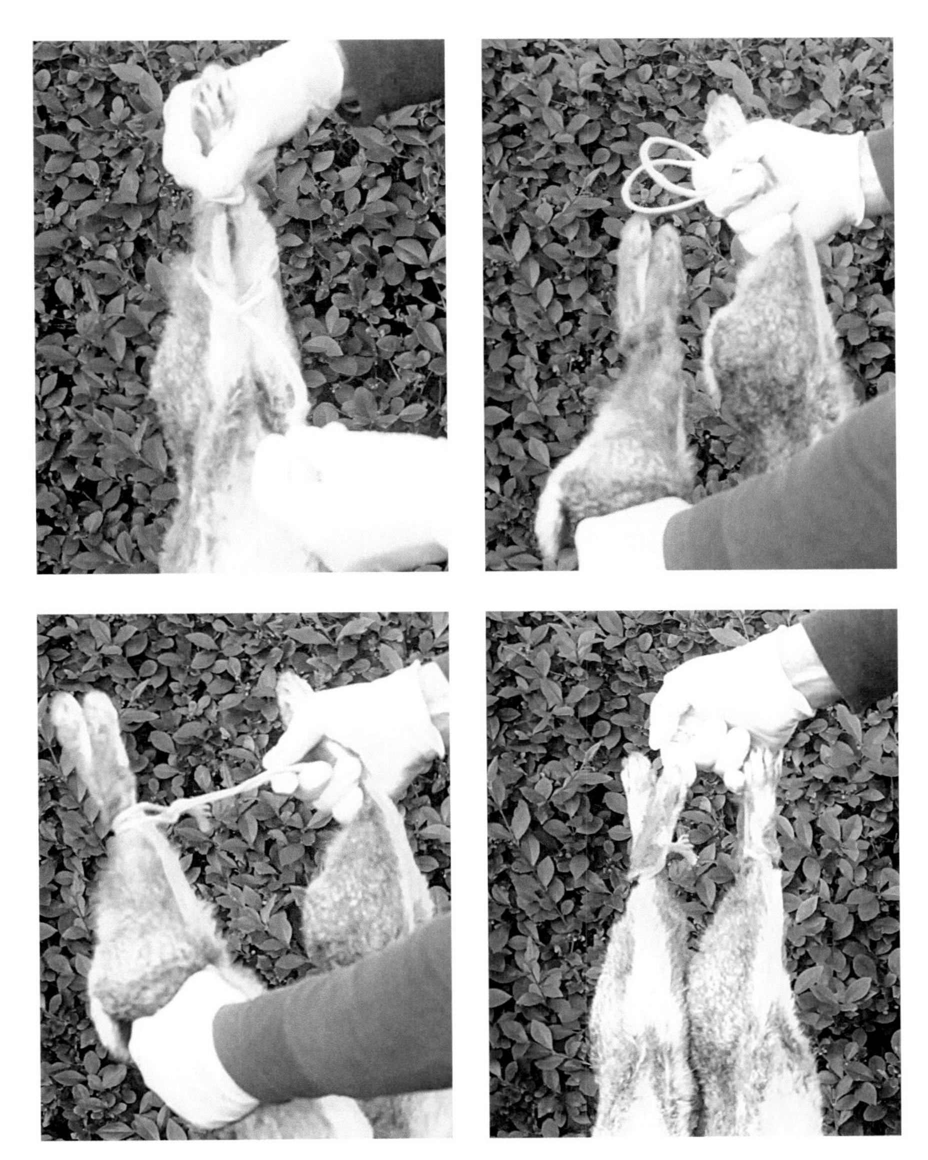

Strings for bracing and aiding carriage

a moment to recover from its exertions. Whilst you are taking care of this chore, your dog will benefit from the break by getting a well-deserved opportunity to get its tongue back in, before you move on to the next field; at such times you will be grateful for having taught your dog to stay (wait), as whilst it is still relatively young and before it has got used to the system, it is likely that it will need to be told to wait for you to be ready. As time goes by, your dog will gradually get used to what is going on and will not need to be told to stay any longer – it will instinctively just wait for you to be ready of its own accord. Then you are starting to build an understanding and are beginning to work as a team.

As the night progresses, you will start to need to think of places where you may stow your catch, as it will start to hinder your movements; getting over gates and through gaps will become very difficult. Eventually, you will have as many braced-up as you can manage, and then the rabbits must stay in the game bag. When that is full, you have no choice but to either leave your catch or stop using the slip lead, thus giving you a spare hand. Life becomes difficult at that moment, but it is the best problem to suffer from during a night's lamping, although it doesn't always feel like it at the time.

You can buy specially made game carriers, which you may like to use instead of strings, but I have never got on with these when rabbiting: the metal used in their manufacture tends to be of a gauge that is not strong enough for rabbits and is inclined to bend; in addition to this, if you jump off a hedge or a bank, rabbits can frequently bounce out of the carrier unnoticed, particularly when it is loaded up to or near capacity. I did have some made for me once out of a much heavier gauge metal rod, but I still didn't particularly like using them; apart from anything else, with the rabbits held in the carriers by their necks, you invariably ended up with rabbit urine all down your side, which did nothing to make the nights seem more enjoyable.

Other people choose to "leg" their rabbits by slitting the skin above the hock sufficiently to thread the second leg through the first, before finishing the job by cutting the second leg on the hock joint so that when lifted it locks into place and cannot become separated. Like this, they can be put on a belt or even legged together in pairs and put over the shoulder without any fear of them separating. Personally, having tried this in the past, I found it to be a perfectly acceptable way of carrying rabbits to a point, but as the number of rabbits being carried increases, so the comfort of carrying them in this way decreases. I now, and have for quite some time, favoured using the simple string method.

Knives

It is always advisable to have a knife in your pocket when lamping; it will come in handy for all manner of unexpected uses and will certainly be required if you do decide to leg your rabbits. It will, of course, become essential at the end of the night when you paunch (remove the entrails) from your catch. The carrying of knives is quite rightly frowned upon in normal everyday life, but nobody is going to question the need for you to carry one whilst you are rabbiting. We don't need any fancy type of knife, just a simple and very basic small penknife that will hold a good edge – this will quite adequately satisfy our needs.

Clothes

Everybody has their own threshold for comfort, but if your plans are to go out and put in a good night's shift, you want to be comfortable, you don't want to get overheated and need to discard and carry clothes, but at the same time you need to make certain provisions. Wellington boots have to be number one – they are a must. Whilst we always hope for windy nights, if we are going to go out on a regular basis we have to accept that not all nights will be favourable to us in terms of weather conditions. The last thing we want on quiet nights are wellies that make excessive noise when we walk; give them a good trial in the shop before you part with your money. Of course, they need to be comfy, but equally, the quieter the better to allow for unfavourable conditions and times where you really need to be silent.

Coats need to be lightweight yet strong, and, of course, waterproof. In addition to this, pay attention to where the coat ends – make sure it is not going to interfere with your dog, who will spend a lot of time right beside you and will not appreciate a coat rubbing against it all night, every night. Pockets in the coat? Are the pockets situated conveniently so that they may hold your strings without the risk of them falling out? Also, will the strings be easy to access when loaded up with battery, bag and previously stringed rabbits? Again, whatever material it is made of, it must be quiet when walking.

Leggings: the right leggings are an asset, I accept, but I just can't be doing with them. To try and find ones that are quiet, strong, waterproof and yet don't make you sweat, without spending a fortune, is for me simply not worth it. I would rather get wet from rain than from sweat, and because of this I have long since not bothered about wearing leggings.

Cap: a cap can be an asset when raining by keeping the rain out of your eyes to an extent, but the difference is marginal and a cap is really a personal preference. At times I have been glad I have one, and at others I have been glad to be rid of it.

Gloves, by their very nature, make everything more difficult to do, but when the wind is howling on the coldest nights, your fingers will be freezing as you hold your lamp up. I find a good compromise on such occasions is to wear fingerless gloves on the really cold nights, when I am always grateful for them, but don't bother with them at any other time.

One final word regarding clothes perhaps should be that you can be absolutely certain that they will become torn and stained relatively quickly, so I would not recommend spending a lot of money unnecessarily on them; personally, I would rather buy two or three sets of average standard and yet suitable attire rather than a single expensive set – by doing this, if you are going out on successive nights, you can always at least start the night dry, no matter how wet your clothes got the night before.

Vehicle

Most people these days have a vehicle, and people's vehicles are often a reflection on what activities the owner participates in. When I first started lamping, I had no vehicle at all. I walked everywhere, but I was fortunate that where I lived gave me immediate access to lamping ground and the need for a vehicle did not exist. Very enjoyable times they were, but as I progressed and became totally obsessed with the pursuit of rabbits by lamping, the need for motor transport became more and more apparent. The result of obtaining this transport meant access to better, more heavily rabbit-populated ground was gained, but an extra significant expense was incurred – something to perhaps consider if your vehicle is to be purely for your sport. If you already have a vehicle – and as previously said, most people do these days – you may well like to consider the type of vehicle you might acquire with lamping in mind. My preference is for a van: I would rather buy an older, cheaper van and not worry about bumping into gateways, scratching the sides and it becoming filthy as a result of night-time excursions, than a better model that gave me constant concern about affecting its condition. The whole nature of what we do and where we go will mean damage, dirt or more than likely both, will affect our vehicles, something to accept right from the start.

With a van, we can construct a comfortable box in the back, within which we can make a comfortable bed of straw for our dogs, who will accept the gesture most gratefully. It is the very least they deserve after a hard night. In the van, we can also easily carry our catch, either hung up on pre-made hooks or, as I prefer, laid out single layered in crates which can be stacked one on top of the other, allowing the air to circulate around them whilst they cool.

Back in my early days when I had no vehicle at all, I recall a friend of a friend who had found out that I went lamping making contact and asking if he could come out with me one night. Sensing an opportunity of travel, an agreement was made that, providing he would drive and collect me for our trip, we had a deal. This he did perfectly in line with our arrangement; however, when we went outside to load up, I could hardly believe my eyes when I realised that he had turned up in a Jaguar with full obligatory leather upholstery! I explained how unsuitable this mode of transport would be and the consequences for the vehicle if we should proceed with our planned excursion, but he insisted that we should, so we duly did. I remember looking into the back seat as we set off and seeing sitting there the little Whippet/Greyhound we were taking out and wondering to myself how many other dogs had travelled to a night's lamping in such luxury! A night to remember, but not something that I could ever recommend as being practical in any way.

Deep Freeze

I have always preferred to sell rabbits fresh and as soon after they have been acquired as possible, typically the morning after they are caught; having a number of butchers ready and prepared to purchase the catch in this way is always to be recommended. Those butchers that want them in the skin can easily be accommodated; those that prefer their rabbits skinned will pay a slightly higher price to reflect this privilege, but there will always be times when either the butchers are temporarily fully stocked or there is a surplus, after all orders have been fulfilled, when you will be left with some. At these times you may need to retain the rabbits longer than you would naturally choose and will, of course, need suitable storage to facilitate this.

The deep freeze is the obvious solution. Rabbits destined for the freezer should be skinned and individually bagged and laid out to freeze in a uniform manner; this way, when they do eventually get sold, even in their frozen state the quality and presentation is high and will look professional.

An additional benefit to having this deep freeze with a constant supply of stock in it will allow you the option of being able to advertise your rabbits for sale to private households, although the numbers sold in this way will almost certainly be much fewer than those the butchers will be prepared to take; they can, of course, be sold at a premium price.

As you become locally known, having proved that you can be relied on to deliver on time supplying rabbits of a high standard, sales will gradually and deservingly increase; this can then become a very profitable way of disposing of your catch.

Occassionally, through absolutely no fault of your dog, a rabbit when skinned may prove to be damaged – perhaps the sheer manner in which it was caught made it impossible for any alternative outcome. These rabbits should never be sold – give them away, joint them and save them for your own consumption, but never sell them. If you are going to lamp regularly and hopefully take high numbers of rabbits, you will need as many outlets as possible; to secure these, you will need a good reputation. It is very short-sighted and damaging to not carry out your own ruthless quality control.

CHAPTER 6
ENTERING

How do we know when a puppy is ready to enter (start work)?

With absolute certainty, if we are honest, we don't, but there are certain physical and behavioural indications that we will start to recognise as the time approaches.

For example, during our normal exercise walks there will be moments where routine games of chase with a sibling – which, up until recently, have just been play – are now being treated more seriously and the game is having to be stopped before things boil over. Play is no longer quite enough, it seems. Pups that have grown up singularly have a tendency to attain a relative maturity earlier; perhaps, with the absence of play and non-participation in games that only puppies seem to know the rules of, this grown-up attitude is unintentionally and unavoidably forced upon them slightly. Physically, the pups' bodies have hardened and their muscles have developed to a level that suggests that they are now equipped with the tools required to attend to their role.

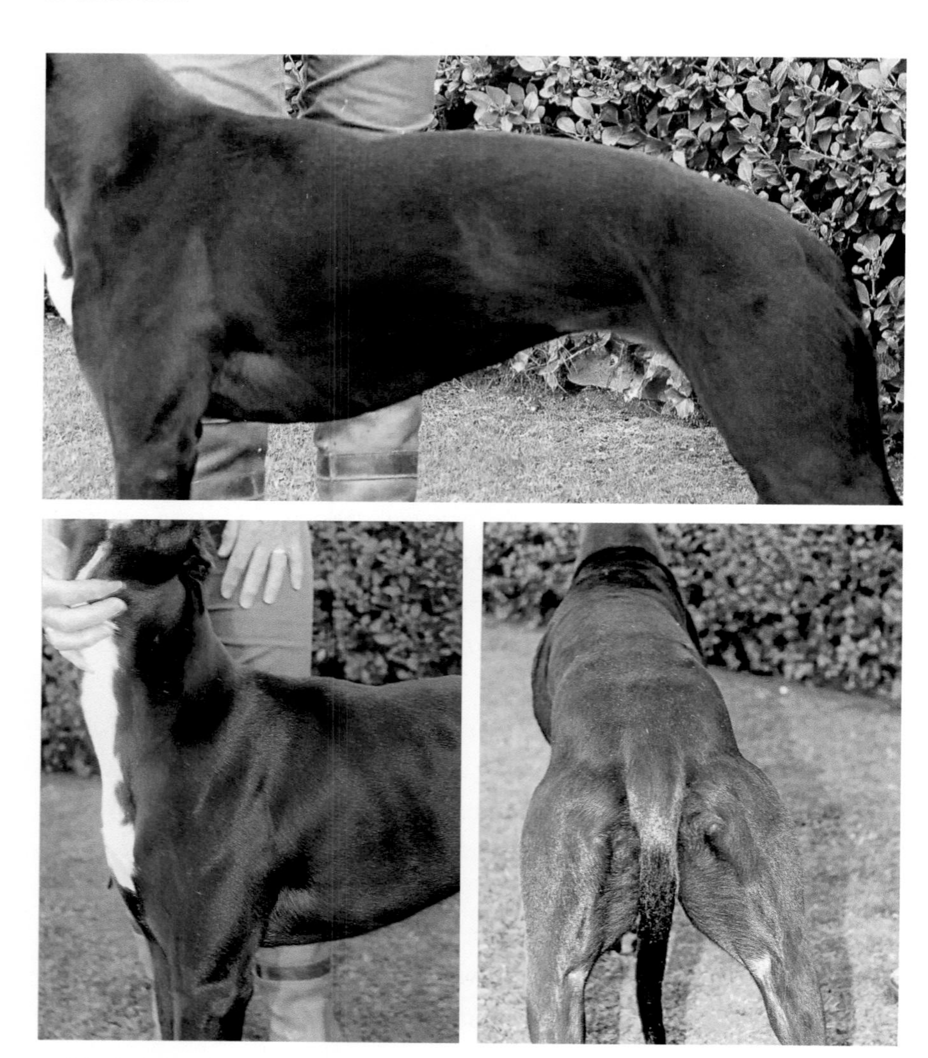

The body has hardened and the puppy is now equipped with the tools to do the job

Perhaps the best indication of all is that you have spent so much time with the pup, getting to know it so well, that you can just feel when it is ready. I realise that this is fine for an experienced person, but what about someone for whom this is their first pup and they are on their own in deciding if the time is right?

For these people, I think the easiest and best advice I could offer would be: if you think your pup is ready and it is younger than ten months, wait; if you think it is ready and it is ten months or over, it probably is; if the pup is ten months and still appears immature, wait longer. This advice is assuming that the type of puppy we are talking about is the type recommended in earlier chapters; this type and size of dog is almost always ready by ten months old. Those people who have alternative views on which type of dog they work and have opted for larger specimens will perhaps need to delay further because, as a general rule, the larger the dog is, the older it will be before it is ready to enter. I have known several dogs that were ruined by being entered prematurely, so do not rush this stage – it will not affect your dog if you hold it back a month or two just to make sure.

You will find other people who will start their puppies much earlier and will be boasting of successes that, at six months old, their dog will do this and their dog will do that. Ignore it. Let them carry on. Don't feel that you are being left behind or need to compete with them. By the time your dog is eighteen months to two years old, you will have a dog of which you will be rightly proud, and see how many of those early starters would gladly swap with you now! It is too late for them – they cannot reverse what they have done or the problems and flaws that they alone are responsible for, but you have years of lamping rabbits ahead of you with a dog that will never be found wanting.

It is perhaps over-simplifying the entering process to just say that with natural mental and physical attributes now apparently present and correct in our pup, it is ready to start; in reality, what we have hopefully achieved is first of all carefully considering the breeding of our pup, then selecting the pup with the apparent correct physique for the job, before most recently training that pup in preparation for its future role. We have now arrived at this important entering stage with a dog whose attitude will have been heavily influenced by our own careful manipulation.

The Greyhound and the Whippet are determined and tenacious. The Collie is much more sensitive than either of the sighthounds. But we have blended the three together, so we have unspecified quantities of each with which to work, but during the pup's development from eight weeks to their current age, we have adjusted ourselves to their individual capabilities, we have not rushed any part of them growing up, we have been patient with the quieter ones and we have insisted that the stronger characters conform, but at all times we have remained fair. We have praised at every opportunity; in fact, we have over-praised at every opportunity; no matter how small each accomplishment may have been, we have made sure that our pups have known how pleased we are and how clever they are. Eight months of applying this type of accolade on our pup and we should now have a pup which not only thinks the absolute world of us, but one which also considers itself to be frankly a bit special. Perfect, exactly what we want: a dog full of confidence and ready to start. What we must do now is to try and keep that confidence intact for as long as possible and get the attitude of being unbeatable ingrained as deep as possible into our pup; it would be futile to have done all the groundwork that we have and then just throw it all away now by not continuing with our careful progress. As written in a previous chapter, we cannot see into a pup's head at eight weeks old in order to pick out the one with the right mentality for the task ahead, but at this, the formative stage of entering, we are still heavily influencing the mental development of our pup; we are still trying to make sure that success is inevitable and failure is a completely unknown state of mind.

When I first started lamping, one dog was never going to be able to satisfy my desire for going out night after night, so I very quickly decided to obtain a second. As unbelievable as it seems now, this was not at all straightforward, but eventually a litter was discovered and the fact it was in the same county was a huge bonus. I had no idea what I was doing or looking at – all I knew was that the pups were Lurchers. One was bought which was a certainty even before I had seen them; it was taught to retrieve as you may expect so soon after accompanying my mentors, but nothing more.

Eventually, she was deemed ready to start. I cannot remember now how old she may have been, but anyway, she was taken out with absolutely no consideration given to anything other than that she should catch rabbits. Rabbits were spotted, the dog was released. Some she saw, some she didn't, but those that were seen were duly missed one after the other, due, in no doubt, to the impossible and unsuitable situations that this young dog had been pushed into. After so many misses, gradually and unsurprisingly this poor young dog lost all confidence in herself and just accepted that she couldn't catch rabbits, so eventually she started to run behind them without ever exerting herself or making any attempt to pick one up. All the blame lay completely and utterly with me – there is no question of that. I feel so sorry now for that poor little dog; falling into my hands at that time was real bad luck for her, with my complete lack of knowledge on how to help and prepare her.

Despite this apparent failure, I was relentless and persevered, so convinced was I that I was doing everything I could; and then one night a complete freak incident saw a rabbit that this dog was ambling along behind get itself caught up in bramble. It panicked and proceeded to make it worse for itself, all of which gave my little dog the opportunity to come slowly along and grab it – she had caught one! Full credit to her: she deserved her slice of luck. That moment had such an effect on her, more than you would think possible. Instantly she believed she could perhaps after all catch rabbits, and she started to put more effort in. She did catch more rabbits, but without doubt, due to my own incompetence she did not catch them consistently enough for me and was very quick to give up when the going got tricky. I had ruined her. Fortunately for me, at least I have an inquisitive mind, and by questioning myself I had come to realise that the fault for her continued poor performances lay completely with me. With the knowledge that I had then gained, as limited as it may have been, I believed I could do things so much better given another opportunity. This little bitch probably taught me more in our short time together than any other dog ever has. I decided our partnership had to end for both our sakes and that I needed to find her a new home. She had a lovely disposition and was soon living with a friend who wanted her as a pet. Occasionally he would take her out lamping, just to let her have a run, and if she caught a couple of rabbits he was overjoyed. How many she didn't catch didn't bother him at all; he kept her for her whole life and she absolutely idolised him.

I quickly learnt, and now know without any possible doubt and would like to share with you that this is absolutely not how to enter a Lurcher to rabbit lamping. I feel ashamed telling this sorry story, but it demonstrates how important confidence in our puppies undoubtedly is; this example makes it absolutely clear that we must preserve the confidence-filled mentality our pups currently have fresh from all of our careful and thoughtfully prepared training.

Other flawed methods of introducing your young dog to lamping include allowing it to come along and watch a more experienced dog in action – the thinking behind this is that it will then copy what the old hand does. I have heard many times people say that they gave their pup "a couple of runs at the end of the night".

I don't care for this at all. First of all, it will mean you will need an accomplice to hold the lead of either your pup or the more experienced dog. Immediately, you are putting faith in someone else who invariably doesn't share your intent or concern in getting everything right. Secondly, the sight of the experienced dog doing its thing will probably have the youngster doing cartwheels on the lead, so desperate will it be to join in. There is also a danger of your youngster "opening up" barking in frustration of being restrained when every bone in its body is telling it to join in. Thirdly, when it becomes the pup's "turn", it is most unlikely due consideration will be applied to the location, and so the chance of any important immediate success is reduced accordingly. In the unlikely event that the "pup's run" does end successfully, we are then expecting it to rush back to us with its catch, where it knows a second higher-ranking dog to be waiting; no pup is ever going to do that, so we have already at this very first stage of entering started to contradict an important element that we want to encourage. I could go on longer, but I suspect you can probably tell I am not in any way a fan of using this method. Yes, I have done this in the past when I knew no better, but now this method, along with, it seems, so many others, is resigned to just being something I used to do.

For me, entering a new puppy has to be a one-man/one-dog session; friends or family who want to see the pup run can wait – this is not the night for them. Tonight we need to concentrate totally on the job in hand;

we don't want any distractions, we want to remain totally focussed on what we are doing.

The night we pick for this exercise will be the darker the better, so completely moonless with as much cloud cover as possible, a fresh to strong wind in the right direction for the ground we are working. Rabbits habitually squat well on a windy night. We want the ground to be soft underfoot but dry: soft enough to offer purchase to the dog if and when turning, yet dry so as not to be slippery.

The fields that we choose must be carefully selected with the pup in mind. In time, when you have found good puppy fields, you may want to wisely resist going in them with your more experienced dogs, who will very quickly reduce the rabbit population in them to zero. No, when you know you have a puppy coming on which is nearly ready to start, save these fields strictly for the puppies only.

When illuminated, rabbits will often squat, as previously said, particularly in the wind, but even more so if they have never been lamped before. These are the rabbits we want for our pup's first attempts. So avoid these puppy fields at all times to give your pup the best chance possible.

Puppy fields? What are they? I call a puppy field one with a relatively flat surface, one that is small enough to be able to lamp the whole field from one spot, thus preventing at any time a rabbit from being able to evade the beam of light, even if it should take an unexpected route, one where all the hedges are solid; better still, a solid-banked bottom with a solid hedge on top. Rabbits need to slow down to gain entry to such a refuge, and with our young pup behind them, they are not afforded such a luxury, so an easy escape is going to have to be earnt. Once a rabbit has been turned – meaning it has been persuaded to change its mind from its initial intentions of where it was going – the advantage swings strongly to our puppy's favour. No barbed-wire. Literally, the very worst that could happen is if we incurred an injury on one of the pup's early runs, so a field where we can easily get between any intended target and the sanctuary that we suspect it will aim for when danger threatens. In doing this on the night, we should be able to get very close to our intended target, and the chances are that if it does bolt for home it will be coming towards us and so make itself fully visible to the pup, who at that moment could easily be looking in the wrong direction, as the beam won't mean anything to it yet. We need a field where the grass is short enough to allow the pup perfect visibility and yet long enough to also encourage the rabbits to sit tight. These are the fields we are aiming for tonight, so that everything is in the dog's favour. If we are careful with our target selection in such a place we have a very high chance of instant success, which is precisely what we are looking for and will continue to look for in our early forays.

So here we are, the big moment we have been waiting for has finally arrived. We have done literally everything possible to make this event a success, so we creep into the field as quietly as possible and, for the first time in our pup's life, we drop the home-made quick-release slip lead over its head. I always love this moment – this could be the start of something special. How will the pup perform? What will its running style be? Will it be brave and crash into hedges? We can't teach that – only its desire to catch overpowering its fear of being hurt will enable it to do that. If it does act like this, its strike rate will improve dramatically. More importantly on this particular night, will it remember what we have taught it and will it behave as we wish? So many questions!

We walk carefully into the position that we have identified as being the one to give our intentions the best chance of success. The lamp goes on and immediately we see that the rabbits are out, and, just as we expected, they are unconcerned by the light. Perhaps the first one or two are not quite positioned where we want them and are immediately rejected as targets; then, suddenly, there he is: a rabbit in the sort of area we had hoped we may find one! The light stays on him and he sinks down into the ground. This is the one for us, but we need to get closer; there is no way our pup would even notice him at this range, let alone have a realistic chance of a catch. All these thoughts rush through your mind as you take a single step towards the intended target, and suddenly he is up and running, but not towards us as we had hoped and anticipated he would – he is running directly away from us. The pressure on the lead informs you that your pup has not even seen it. This is not the rabbit for us after all. But there is another just to the side of where the last one had been. This one will do equally well, and we can see by the way his ears have gone down flat that he is not intending to move any time soon; so, before we commit to this new target, we have a quick scan around to see if there are any other, perhaps even better, targets. There are others, but much farther away – they are not concerned or apparently even aware of our presence, so we will leave them where they are for now and concentrate on this previously identified potential target. We leave the light on him as we move towards him. He wriggles right down flat and he is sure we haven't seen him. As we get closer, he is now perfect for us. Start to whisper your sound or command to "fetch"; the lead goes tight, but do not be tempted to release your pup, hold it back. The lead may have gone tight because of your command, it may have gone tight because the wind catching the dock leaf behind the rabbit has interested your pup; it is far more likely that whatever has increased your pup's interest levels, it is not the obvious rabbit in the centre of the beam – it will be almost certain that this is yet to be noticed. We are now standing ten yards from where the rabbit is. He is right in the middle of the illuminated circle, so do not be tempted to release the pup. Should you fall to that temptation, the most likely outcome would be the dog running past the rabbit towards the dock leaf. As the dog passes the rabbit, the noise will cause it to bolt, and your pup will probably not even detect the rabbit's presence and a perfectly set-up scenario will very quickly become wasted.

Still the rabbit remains motionless, but we are as close now as we want to be; stand still and keep the light on your target and tap one of your boots against the other. This unexpected new sound is very likely to encourage the rabbit to lift its ears, maybe just one, but this movement could be all that we need. Suddenly, the lead is really tight now: we are certain the dog is looking at what we want it to be looking at. One more step towards the rabbit and immediately it is up and away. The pup lunges in response, so release the cord and your pup is running. Towards the hedge they go, pup gaining ground predictably. As they reach the hedge, the rabbit does not feel able to slow down to enter the solid hedge; it knows to just throw itself in, as weaker hedges would permit entry. In this situation, however, it would be suicide so it does all it can under the circumstances and sets off running down the hedge line. Our pup is in hot pursuit, when suddenly the rabbit turns in its own body length and our dog continues on. Ignore the dog; keep the light on the rabbit and the dog will turn and hopefully rejoin the chase. Then your pup is back in the beam, having recovered the ground, and is once more closing in and threatening the rabbit. This time the rabbit throws caution to the wind, attempts to enter the hedge, falters, and the pup reacts perfectly and suddenly it has the rabbit in its mouth – it has caught its first run. Forget the rest of the field, and don't worry about disturbing the rest of the rabbits – they don't matter now. Call your dog excitedly, encourage it to come straight back as fast as possible. If all goes well, it will do exactly that and deliver its first catch. Take the still very much alive rabbit, dispatch it and place it into the bag. Praise the dog like never before, as if it has done the cleverest thing imaginable, and it will almost certainly be beside itself with joy.

That's it for tonight. Stop. Continue to praise the dog every few steps, leave it in no doubt as to how clever it is, but resist the temptation to try for another rabbit. Leave it where you are; there is nothing to be gained by catching another – that would just leave you back where you are already. But if your pup missed the next run, what would you do then? Try another and then perhaps another? The risk is far too high of undoing all the good you have done and losing the feeling of achievement and success that your pup currently holds. No, stop now, enjoy the moment and let your dog digest the night undefeated. I have been fortunate to have been in this position more times than I care to mention, but trust me, the excitement of your dog's first catch never lessens; it means so much. It may be just a single rabbit, but it is the first. Hopefully you will reach many landmarks together – first squatter, first double figures, first who knows what? – but there will not be a single rabbit that this dog will ever catch that will individually mean so much or be so important to you or your dog's progress as the first one. One swallow does not make a summer, but one rabbit will be seen to make a massive difference to your dog.

This imaginary scenario, were it to come true, would be the perfect start for any Rabbit Lamping Lurcher. Much of the example given is in our own hands: if we choose carefully and plan meticulously, we can create an opportunity in line with this description. Having set up this seemingly simple opportunity for our young dog, despite the odds being heavily shortened in our favour, much can still go wrong.

On approaching our rabbit, it may have decided that it isn't moving, so convinced is it that it has remained unnoticed. Approaching as we are from the direction that we expect the rabbit to run, we do not want to get any closer than the approximately ten yards that we are currently at; if the rabbit bolted from here and came back towards us, the dog will clearly be sighted and the run will be on. However, if we walk right up to the rabbit and the dog is still not sure where exactly the rabbit is, when it does bolt we will be right on top of it. Everything will take place so near that with the lamp at the angle it will be and the dog sensing the moment, before you know it the rabbit has gone and the dog is left both unsighted and completely bewildered as to what has just occurred, so once we have reached ten yards, I would recommend, if we are still at this *status quo* and our rabbit is sitting tight, we move out to the right-hand side of the rabbit. Retain the approximate ten-yard gap between you and slowly circle the rabbit. If your dog is like mine, it would be in your left hand; by going to the right if at any moment the rabbit bolts for home, your dog has clear visibility and you have not positioned yourself to have unintentionally become an obstacle. If at any moment the rabbit bolts, the dog will be away and the run is on. If it does not and you manage to do a complete semi-circle around the squat target, now and only now we can walk closer to it. It is now, by shepherding the rabbit towards home, more than likely that we will get a bolt very soon as the rabbit's nerve eventually gives way. Do not, under any circumstances, allow the dog to try and take it from this squat position – later in life this will be exactly what we want our dog to accomplish, but that is not for tonight. Attempting that at this delicate moment is almost certain to end with the rabbit being missed. Apart from the strong chance of things going completely wrong in attempting a squatter at this stage, in the extremely unlikely event of the dog being successful, we would put ourselves in the strange position of having caught our first rabbit without fulfilling the lesson that tonight has been designed for. No, tonight is for moving targets only, and at this moment we have got ourselves into a position that is absolutely impossible to improve on in which to slip a young Rabbit Lamping Lurcher.

So if your continued approach is still not enough to make the rabbit bolt, this is not impossible, though incredibly unlikely. If necessary, touch the rabbit with your foot; nothing jerky, just touch it as if your foot was moving to achieve a normal slow walking step. Now when the rabbit bolts – and if you do get this far it definitely will now bolt – it is in clear view for your dog. Without any fear of the dog being unsighted, you have not got in the dog's way yourself and the run is on from that point on. You are no longer manipulating the situation; the pup must now step up to the plate. Let's hope that the conclusion of the run goes along the lines of the imaginary scenario given, and because of the care that you have taken in presenting the pup with this opportunity, there is an extremely high chance that it will indeed do just that.

However, your rabbit may have very different ideas on how this run is going to conclude. The run could still end without the catch that we really were hoping for. Should this unfortunately happen, do not despair, but concentrate on what you are doing – despair later! At this moment, encourage your dog back to you. Get it to return as quickly as possible; do not give it time to even consider putting its nose down and self-hunting – that would make a disappointing outcome even worse.

If our dog has missed but returned, as it definitely will, having been trained correctly, we are still in a position to offer much praise. We don't have a catch, but our dog has done everything it could and returned to hand in the appropriate manner. If our encouragement to our dog to return has disturbed the remaining rabbits in the field, we care not. Tonight is not all about catching rabbits; there are still benefits to be taken, and we will just move on to the next suitable field that we had earmarked for such an eventuality.

If the first attempt ended fruitless, I would certainly attempt a second if the right situation can be found again. All of the above precautions should be adhered to and hopefully this time we can enjoy a more positive outcome. In the event of success just like in our imaginary scenario, praise and praise again before heading for home.

Should you really be unlucky and once again fail to attain a catch, make sure your dog comes straight back to hand as before, praise him and then head for home. Your dog will have enjoyed the experience; it should not have been too badly affected by its failed attempts. Try again on another night – that is literally the only option available to us. If we carry on tonight and risk missing more, we will be in danger of the dog becoming frustrated, which may well affect its initial confidence; it may even, in the absolute worst case, open up (bark), and that's the last thing we would want to happen. The most likely outcome will be that on another night success will be gained and tonight's disappointments will quickly be forgotten. By far the more likely outcome is that with such careful choice of where this exercise takes place and which run we select, instant success will have been enjoyed.

With our young dog likely to have completed its first catch, we will be called upon to despatch the rabbit as quickly and as humanely as we possibly can. Simply hold the rabbit in one hand and, with your second hand under its chin, quickly twist the head up and jerk it back and this will disconnect the neck; or holding the rabbit in the same position as just described, twist the head one way and the body firmly the other – again death will be instant and the never-pleasant task completed.

We now have our young dog with a catch to its credit. The pup has no idea of what a fabricated situation it was put into and confidence will be high; this is exactly what we have strived for, but now we need to repeat this exercise, taking the same amount of care in selecting both location and target – the longer we can continue without a miss, the better. If we were able to go out perhaps three times with a one-run/one-catch ratio, this would be perfect; but on the third or fourth night, if all has gone well, I would certainly consider trying for a second. Exactly the same procedure would be followed. It is impossible to be too careful, so go alone and always make sure the dog comes straight back to you quickly after a catch or a miss. If you were able to get the numbers of runs your dog has had on various nights up to ten without a miss, you – or perhaps it is fairer to say your dog – have done exceptionally well; even in these selected conditions, to achieve ten catches without a miss, you need to wrap that dog up carefully: it is a bit special.

Eventually, of course, your dog will have a miss. The longer we go without one the better, but miss it most surely will. This can be a very revealing moment, particularly for pups that have enjoyed repeated success. The moment that the pup realises that the run it has just been on, that it almost certainly was expecting to be another formality, has, in fact, ended without a catch, it is now in unchartered territory. It has never been here before, so you will need to allow a brief moment just to be sure that the rabbit has indeed gained safety and is not about to reappear, as they often will at such times. During this moment, there is nothing I like more than to see a pup look back at me. I interpret that glance, no matter how fleeting, to be a combined mixture of shock – so sure was it that it was going to achieve yet another catch – but also for the first time the pup is wondering, what do I do now? Whilst in this train of thought, its natural instinct has led it to look back at me for possible guidance. It sees me as its partner – we are in it together – and these are the moments that make working with a dog so special for me. If other people, perhaps with other dogs, were present at those moments, they wouldn't happen, and even if they did, they may go unnoticed; they certainly wouldn't have the same impact or level of meaning. You have started to form a bond. Call your dog back and make a fuss of it; it has learnt an important lesson: lamping rabbits is not quite as easy as it first appeared to be. I guarantee the next run your dog has you will see a more determined dog with an even higher degree of effort being applied; having initially decided that rabbits were easy due to its immediate success and perhaps becoming a little complacent, it now knows differently. Your dog has proved by its earlier catches that it is up to the job; now it has graduated to realising that full effort is required at all times; this is the moment when your dog takes a big step forward. It has learnt that the same rule of "you get out what you put in" applies to it as well. We can take a little bit of satisfaction and pat ourselves on the back at this point for having helped our dog get to this stage in this frame of mind and really start to look forward to the future dark nights that lie ahead.

This, for me, is absolutely the right way to enter a puppy to lamping rabbits. It eliminates as much chance of failure as is humanly possible. If I was advising anybody, particularly someone inexperienced, how to get the best possible start for their Rabbit Lamping Lurcher, those would be precisely the steps I would strongly recommend. I have arrived at this method after trying various ways over a long period of time and found that, for me, it works every time. Each dog will have their own individual characteristics to interpret, but despite this the system remains consistent and the results it provides likewise.

However, every so often – very, very rarely – a pup comes along and you just know right from the start, right from its very first run, that it is a bit different, a complete natural, and a cut above the rest. In my forty years-plus of lamping rabbits with Lurchers, I have perhaps been blessed with two that stood out in this way. Whilst on their first run you just immediately knew there was only ever going to be one outcome; both treated it like they had been doing it for years, and both appeared to instinctively know what to expect and how to react. I must confess that on both occasions I broke my own rules and did not restrict either pup to just one run.

The first was way back in 1996, the second was in much more recent times. In my defence, I can claim to have experience on my side, and both times I was proved correct: they were both definitely a cut above the rest when it came to lamping rabbits. The first took four out of four in her first field on her first night and just had a complete air of not having done anything in particular – it was really no problem to her. I found the rabbits, she went and got them. Simple! What's the big deal? It was so enjoyable, and in truth surprising, to see just what was actually possible. She reminded me that we never stop learning ourselves; we tend to focus so much on teaching our canine partners that sometimes we overlook our own limitations. That particular bitch, as easy as she found routine runs, would also risk her life rather than let a rabbit escape. We would never want our dogs to lose their life or even get injured, but equally we can only marvel at this application to their role. Those two dogs were definitely exceptions, of that there is no doubt; we cannot expect their kind to come along very often. If you are blessed with one, savour every moment – you may never have another.

Pups entered in the way previously described will bring more than satisfactory results, and just because our standard pups are not blessed with such rare natural talent does not mean that, with our help and tuition, they will not attain or at least approach that incredibly high standard in the future.

Our pups now know exactly what their role is to be and will be prepared to take on the world, so confident they will have become. We need to preserve that confidence, but also gradually relax our protective attitude towards them; they need to be allowed to develop their skills in ever-increasingly hard places for them to achieve a catch. We must remain careful at all times to stay within the capabilities of our dogs during these early nights, just as with their earlier basic training, but equally we must try to help them develop, whilst not unduly holding them back. A real tall order and difficult to achieve combination, as each pup will be different; everybody has different ground on which to work, so there cannot be a single path to follow. Take progress slowly; as your dog's performances inspire more confidence, you alone will know which runs to allow it to attempt and which are those it would be better to pass by.

My tendency at this transitional stage between entering the pup and it becoming a full-blown member of the rabbiting team is to now reverse what we have previously done; instead of habitually finding an easy rabbit for the pup, I routinely now gradually relax the level of difficulty of runs attempted but revert to an "easy" run (if such a thing really exists) if my dog has suffered a couple of misses. Never allowing a long period to develop between catches is, I find, sufficient precaution with a sapling when coupled with the dog's natural enthusiasm to protect the all-important confidence previously attained. Following these measures, your dog will gradually improve; it will gain running fitness and with quite rapid progress will soon be ready to take on a full, unrestricted night's work.

One final word before leaving this chapter would be to remember that there are no rules. Don't rush: graduate at the pace that you think is right for your dog and your dog alone.

CHAPTER 7
LAMPING

It is a very strange sentiment that farmers habitually like to moan about the number of rabbits on their land. The sight of two or three rabbits sitting in the sun up a hedgerow, in a farmer's mind, is proof that they are overrun, with the situation often being described as a plague! Yet enquiries about being given permission to catch these rabbits on their behalf free of charge and rid them of their worries are met with instant refusal. This has never and will never make any sense, but all too disappointingly it is the way it so often is for us lampers.

This unfortunate reality is a problem that the average Lamping person must overcome in order to be able to pursue their interest.

In truth, many rabbit lamping people poach; this is not right and it is illegal, but unfortunately it is also understandable. Much has been written about these poaching lampers and how they cause destruction wherever they go. This does not quite sit well with me, as logically I cannot imagine that anyone illegally lamping would want to betray their own trespass by causing any damage. All the rabbit lampers I have met, some through friendship and some through actually catching them red-handed poaching on estates where I have worked as a Gamekeeper, whether they lamped legally or otherwise, their intentions were to go and catch rabbits – nothing more, nothing less. Damage nothing and have as much respect for property and stock as if it were their own. To the unknowing, the idea of trespassers having respect for the property they quite illegally go on may sound too good to be true, but consider it logically: if you had permission, why would you jeopardise it by causing any damage? Equally, if you didn't have permission, any damage caused would only signify to a probably completely unaware farmer that someone was trespassing on his land. The next time a light illuminated his bedroom, instead of turning over and thinking he was dreaming, he would almost certainly get up and come out. Why would you risk that when, with a little care, it could be so easily avoided? Your illegal yet overlooked activities could then continue in the future.

It is undoubtedly better to have permission to work the ground you are on. Your mind can stay focussed on the job in hand, there would be no need to keep looking over your shoulder, and I am certain that the whole experience will be far more enjoyable. So how could someone obtain permission? Depending on who you know, perhaps even who your friends or family know, this could be extremely easy; for others with no direct or even indirect contact with the farming community, it could be extremely difficult.

Personally, the most direct approach of simply knocking on farmhouse doors and politely asking the question has rarely been met with a favourable response for me. Whether I don't have the right manner or whether farmers just can't handle such a direct, straightforward question, I have never been able to determine, but whatever the reason may be, this approach has so very rarely worked for me.

Advertising yourself by means of notices in local papers, markets and agricultural suppliers can sometimes work and is always worth a try.

Harvest and Lambing times can be good occasions to appear and offer help by knocking on the door and leaving your telephone number, should any help be required at this busy time (it almost certainly will be). Once you make the farmer's acquaintance, your chances have immediately improved; now you can play him at his own game and after having proved to him that you are reliable and trustworthy, having got to know him a little, you can pick precisely the right moment to ask the question with the optimum chance of a favourable response.

Gamekeepers, too, so long the arch-rival of the poaching fraternity, are invariably busy at various times of the year and would appreciate a hand from the right sort of trustworthy person. The best opportunity to get in with one would be to appear just before the shooting season and offer your assistance as a beater; be regular, be reliable, and doors will open. Gamekeepers often hold the key to thousands of acres. Whilst you are beating, you will almost certainly be rubbing shoulders with people from the farming community from the surrounding area; be sure to be close to them at soup time and gradually make their acquaintance – you have a whole shooting season to get what you are after. Many of them will enjoy shooting themselves, but once you have proved yourself trustworthy you will find that even these people are not overly protective of their rabbit population. The most important thing on securing permission is to make absolutely certain of your boundaries – upsetting your farmer's neighbour will be the quickest and easiest method of ruining all that groundwork, and you will very quickly lose your treasured privilege.

Once you have started to achieve your goal of being granted access to any land, the sheer fact that you have permission will then almost certainly lead to more as you prove that you can be trusted, you do a good job, you are quiet, efficient and fully compliant to any conditions that may have been attached. Farmers talk particularly to their neighbours; they may not like them, but they talk to them! The fact that one saw a light on the other's ground last night will not go unmentioned, and immediately you are being talked about – perhaps not the first or even the second time you get mentioned – but on one of these occasions it will be suggested your farmer may like to send you around to look at the second farmer's land with a view to keeping his rabbits under control as well, and so it begins. You are in!

You may be asked to demonstrate that your dogs are not going to kill every sheep for miles around as a final condition to permission being granted; this is a perfectly reasonable concern on the farmer's behalf – if you consider the roles reversed, you would want assurance that the dogs you were allowing onto your land could be trusted with your stock, so it should not be a problem for us to demonstrate that our dogs are indeed totally reliable. You will then be able to take reward from the farmer's response when he realises that actually our dogs are twice as obedient as his own. He will have heard tales of Lurchers – invariably bad, exaggerated stories – but he will not expect the demonstration that you are able to give him.

Once you have permission, if you always remain mindful of how difficult it was to obtain and yet how easy it could be to lose by not being respectful, there is no reason why you should not be able to enjoy access to that area of land for life.

However you have managed to obtain permission – and in truth even if you haven't – it is most important that you should walk around it in daylight hours first before lamping it at night. Apart from the obvious things of interest to us, such as rabbit buries and general signs of rabbit activity, there will be much more that we need to take in on these reconnaissance missions. Gateways and gaps in hedges that permit passage from one field to another must be memorised; it is surprising how good you will become at doing this over a period of time and how accurate you will get at aiming towards them from distance in the dark. As you go, you will start to plan your route based on what you find, wherever possible always remembering to try to achieve getting between feeding rabbits and where they will aim for when danger threatens, and particularly where there are the heaviest signs of rabbit activity.

The most important matter by far on these visits is to identify any particular threat of danger to your dog. Habitually, farmers will leave old, broken or just simply abandoned farm machinery lying in corners of fields and other odd places; sheep troughs, cattle feeders (or parts of) must all be noted; any of these could lead to serious injury or in the worst cases, ultimately death to a running dog.

Typical natural danger to a dog running the hedge at night

Important to be aware of these kinds of dangers before setting out at night

For me, too much danger in one area and the risk of injury or even worse is far too high. Despite this farm being lamped many, many times, this area is always avoided at night. Risk for reward does not add up

Barbed-wire and electric fences must also be noted; again, both can cause severe injury or worse to our dogs.

I recall on one particular occasion where the lamping session, as per normal for this particular farm, was preceded by a mug of tea with the farmer and his wife in the farmhouse kitchen. Having set off on one of the first rabbits of the night, the little bitch that I was running came to a sudden abrupt halt. The howls made it clear something was badly wrong. She was below me at the bottom of a steep field, so I ran down to her and could quickly see that she had become trapped in a coil of barbed-wire, and her injuries looked extensive and serious. With difficulty working alone, I freed her from the barbed-wire and carried her back to the van. Fortunately, her wounds were not as bad as first feared, but despite this she did require extensive stitching. It came to light that the farmer and his team had been constructing a new fence, and where they had finished for the day they had left the remaining wire from the roll at the edge of the field. This is what my little dog had run into; why he had not had the presence of mind to let me know that this was so whilst we had our mug of tea, I don't know, but it demonstrates the dangers our dogs face. That particular story had a happy ending in that the injured dog was soon back at work and, other than rather ugly scars, she was none the worse for her nasty experience.

On another occasion, I was running a really promising young bitch who already had several catches to her name. Despite being extremely promising, she was still very much in the early stages of learning her trade. She was running a rabbit on this particular night and as it reached the hedge, she dived in after it; the squeal of the rabbit betrayed the fact that she had been successful, but that was very quickly followed by a howl from the dog, who reappeared without her catch and circled around me, reluctant to come to me. Eventually she did, but on inspection I could see no damage to her and for a brief moment thought that she must have just twisted something or caught herself on an object which had led to no visible injury. However, on turning my attention to the hedge, I could now see that a two-strand electric fence had been constructed beside the hedge; clearly by its height, it was intended to contain sheep, and the wire was unusually dark and had been invisible before closer inspection.

That young bitch never caught another rabbit in her whole life. I tried and tried every conceivable thing I could think of to get her back on track, but I became certain that she had convinced herself that the rabbit had caused the shock she had suffered, and she was never prepared to risk it happening again. She got back to the stage of running the rabbits, but she would not even attempt to pick one up. She would not even any longer retrieve a dead rabbit, and that single unfortunate incident ruined her for life.

So, anything that could possibly cause a problem for your dog should be memorised; drains, ditches, tree stumps, the list is endless, but any time spent locating and remembering them is never wasted.

Rabbit Lampers are not restricted – as many other sportsmen are – by when they can take their quarry; there is no close season, as rabbits are classed as pests as opposed to Game. However, if your intention is to enjoy your sport, each year you will not want to totally eradicate all the rabbits from your ground, so whilst keeping numbers under control to justify any permission being granted, you must leave a breeding stock to replenish what you have taken away. Rabbits being rabbits, they are very good at this and the speed at which the numbers return, even though you expect and understand it will happen, still somehow manages to surprise.

For several years I concentrated on a self-imposed "season" of September through the winter months to March, and while still occasionally lamping outside these months, particularly on request, this was for me the Lamping season. When and how that season came into effect I can't honestly remember, but I think it was close enough. Now I believe for my home area (Devon), the months should perhaps move one month earlier; I find that I catch far more milky does in March than I do in August. So now in August, or as soon as the Harvest is in and the ground is soft enough (for the dogs' feet), I start lamping, bringing the season to a conclusion now at the end of February/early March, starting the season being always so much easier to do than stopping. This gives us seven full months in which to work the dogs.

During these seven months you will encounter most if not all of Britain's weather conditions and, of course, every moon phase possible. When I first started Lamping, I quickly became totally obsessed and would lamp night after night after night, totally oblivious of weather conditions or the phase of the moon; eventually, when being out alone at night became the norm, this initial madness passed and it started to dawn on me that there were certain times and conditions within which I would do just as well banging my head against a brick wall as to go lamping rabbits. I guess, looking back, that moment was perhaps when I first started trying to perfect something that by its very nature must always remain imperfect.

Full moons are not the nights for lamping rabbits; they are undoubtedly some of the most beautiful nights to be out walking in, but with regards to helping us with what we are trying to do, they are non-starters. By lamping in the full moon we are tipping the scales strongly in the rabbit's favour; lamping on these nights will result in an unacceptably high number of unsuccessful runs, a real confidence battering for your dog, and as if that wasn't enough, you will have educated the rabbits in that area to the lamp, which will have a detrimental effect on your night's sport when you return later in more favourable conditions. Two weeks out of every four the moon phase becomes ideal for lamping rabbits: dark nights. In addition to this, we can gain a further five or six partial nights by going out early on a falling moon or late on a rising moon. On all of these more favourable moon phases you have a realistic chance of a successful night's sport, provided the moon phases have coincided with the right weather conditions.

Obviously, frost and ice totally rule out Lamping Rabbits; even if the noise you make just walking wasn't enough (which it is), the prospect of running your dog on such ground is totally unacceptable – the chances of broken toes and burnt-off or grazed pads injuries that seem to take forever to heal are so high that lamping in these conditions is a definite no. I appreciate living in Devon I am luckier than many with regards to these types of weather conditions; when we do get them, more often than not they coincide with the full moon, so we are often spoilt by getting rid of our most unfavourable conditions at the same time.

Rain: I know lampers who consider rainy nights to be unsuitable for lamping rabbits, but I believe the truth to be closer to rainy nights being unsuitable for some lampers! As the saying goes, "it is better to have a poor excuse than none at all". The simple fact is, whilst it must be agreed that some nights are totally unacceptable for lamping rabbits, if we wait for only the perfect nights our lamping trips are going to be severely restricted. Rain does nothing to improve the enjoyment of the night, nor does it improve the chances of finding high numbers of rabbits out feeding, but you can still have successful nights in such weather conditions if you persevere. I have once – and only once, to my recollection – been out in a storm where it rained so hard that no rabbits were found in a location that was known without doubt to hold high numbers, so I will concede that it is possible for rain to ruin a night to the point of being a waste of time, but that would only happen very, very rarely, and even then, if you were tenacious enough, it would be most unlikely to last all night.

Wind, on the other hand, is the lamper's friend: it hides the sound of your approach, it hides the sound of the dogs running, other rabbits being caught, the opening and closing of gates and any other unfavourable sounds you can think of. If we were to be asked to put in an order for the conditions we would like for Lamping Rabbits with Lurchers, there would be no moon, the temperature would be above freezing, it would be dry and the wind would be blowing. If you get a dry, windy night that follows a particularly wet night, these are often the best nights of all. I have often gone out in such favourable conditions and found that the numbers of rabbits out feeding far exceeded those that I had actually believed to have been in any particular area.

On many nights during the course of our "season" the moon phase will be right, but it will not be accompanied by any wind at all, not even a breeze; it could be drizzling or perhaps have intermittent showers, and all of these weather conditions are acceptable whilst not being perfect for lamping rabbits with Lurchers. On these nights the behaviour of the rabbits is more likely to determine the level of success we enjoy. Nervous, perhaps lamp-shy rabbits can prove extremely hard to catch in these conditions, where, if the wind was blowing hard, good numbers could be taken from exactly the same area. In less favourable weather conditions, good numbers can be taken in areas where the rabbits have not been disturbed before or at least enough to make them shy. You will gradually learn which conditions suit which of your places, and if you remain flexible, letting the conditions decide for you where best to go on any particular night, your end-of-season numbers caught will be your just reward.

Another factor that will have an enormous effect on any lamping trip is the type of ground that you lamp on. In my area of Devon, the majority of farms have a tendency to be relatively small and mixed usage; others, I appreciate, having myself worked in the Midlands, the North of England and in Scotland, are completely different. Generally speaking, each will have factors that make life easier for us and each will have things that make life more difficult; it is up to us to interpret how best to adapt to the ground we have and how best to approach it.

Whatever the type of ground we have to work, our biggest help and the biggest hindrance in our efforts for success are undoubtedly the field boundaries. This is where the majority of our action will take place; as mentioned in chapter 6 ("Entering"), flat pasture in small fields with solid boundary hedges are what we want and I believe is all they have in heaven. Here on earth we are all too frequently confronted with anything but that perfect combination. We have fields that go downhill to a wood with nothing but a single strand of barbed-wire separating the two; for me they are the worst. We have fields that have not had the hedges trimmed for years and so now have perhaps six foot of bramble and saplings growing around the headland – difficult, but with a dog that is brave, confronted with cover we can make it work. We have fields with loose hedges and those that are stock-fenced; in these areas, when a rabbit reaches the boundary, it could go either way – here a dog efficient at picking up early in the open will help us most. We have stone walls which are a great barrier to help us, but then invariably have fallen stones along their length – these can easily cause our dog an injury. Where I live, there is a lot of coastal ground with gorse banks, allowing the rabbits an easy escape route to dive into.

Why can't all hedges be like this?

The worst! The single strand wire leading straight into the wood. The greenery that at first glance appears to be a hedge is, in fact, rhododendron growing in the wood rooted about 8ft below the level of the field's surface – an absolute nightmare for the rabbit lamper – and any catch here is either very, very clever or very lucky. A place perhaps better revisited with a long net and keep the dog's confidence intact

Stone wall with the normal fallen stones creating a serious danger to the lamping dog

Nothing much stopping the rabbits running straight in here except a real brave and determined lunge which, with Whippet-type skin and the sharply angled gorse stems, could easily and often will lead to injury

So much variation to which we must adapt. Some farms will have within their boundaries a little bit of each of these and perhaps more; on these farms we need to be particularly versatile in how we decide to deal with all the different combinations we are confronted by. Our first few visits to these places may not be overly successful until we have worked out the best route and how to get the best out of any particular area of ground we have to work.

The golden rule is to always try to have the rabbits coming back towards you whenever possible. There are several very good reasons for this; for example, if the rabbits come back towards you, the run will conclude very close to where you are positioned and the dog hasn't got far to go to deliver its catch and be ready to go again. Another example would be if you imagine perhaps half a dozen rabbits feeding in relatively close proximity on a windy night – by taking the nearest target first, which, as we have said, will come back towards you as soon as it passes you, your light will now be shining directly away from the other preoccupied rabbits, which will quite likely continue feeding untroubled. Having secured the first, we can now repeat this process as many times as possible; it won't always go perfectly, but I think it can be seen how advantageous this arrangement can be when it does go right. In addition to these obvious benefits, consider for a moment if you lamped the same group of rabbits from the other side of where they are feeding, when your dog ran it would invariably take on the nearest first; approached in this manner this rabbit, when disturbed, is going to almost certainly spook at least some of the others, if not all, and should the dog fail to get a quick pick-up, turning the rabbit up and down the hedge line means that from your position on the far side of the rabbits you are going to be constantly lamping any other rabbits that have decided to continue feeding. Then, on conclusion of the run, whether successful or not, the dog is going to return to you again through or past any rabbit crazy enough to still be feeding, which almost certainly will put paid to the whole group. If this initial run has proved unsuccessful, you could easily end up with no rabbit at all to show for your efforts, as opposed to a realistic prospect of taking three or four out of the group of six the former way. It is most certainly not impossible that you may get them all. I have done this type of thing on many occasions, but usually, under routine circumstances, you would be happy with three or four. Achieve this a few times during the course of the night and the number in the bag will be significantly higher than it would have been without your reconnaissance and forward planning.

With regards to using the lamp, each person will have their own method. As hard as it seems to believe with a discipline that basically has two stages – either on or off – how you apply your personal methods with the lamp will make a massive difference to your success. How you lamp the rabbits will determine the number of runs you get. Do you consider the dog or just hope for the best? Right down to the amount of time the lamp is actually on: if you are out for the night each battery has its limit, and battery power must never be wasted. If the way you are lamping feels awkward, change it; there are no rules – develop your own system. If, like me, you prefer your own company, any time you may lamp with someone else, especially if they use the lamp, you will find it most frustrating. I remember lamping with one person one night (and one night only!), there was absolutely no way that you could predict where the light would shine next – it was all over the place, to the left, to the right, back to the left again; it was impossible to keep up and was totally impractical. Strangely, his dog was quite good and seemed to have adapted to this shall we say unorthodox technique far better than you would ever have expected it to. The one good thing that comes from nights such as these is that it reminds me why I lamp alone.

Nobody can really say what is the right way to use the lamp, but it is perfectly obvious that you need a system whereby you can be reasonably sure that you have checked each field thoroughly without incurring unnecessary battery power wastage. How long you actually leave the light on for and how long the distance you walk in that field before each check will be determined by the type of field you are in. Stubble and longer grass always needs more careful inspection, as will grass fields with a heavy weed growth; others, for example recently germinated winter wheat, can be far more easily checked. I find the best place to start on entering a field is to whichever side of the gateway has the longest distance to the corner of the field; most gateways have a tendency to be towards a corner of the field for obvious herding reasons, so starting on the longer side, I swing steadily around the field in one continuous arc. If a rabbit is spotted close by and is already on the move, I immediately slip the dog; if there is no immediate sign of rabbits or any that may be there are not worried about the lamp, I would continue checking the field, leaving them for later. As you scan, your mind will instinctively be working out how best to work the field on this particular night. As quickly as your assessment develops, so it can change with each new revelation that the lamp reveals. Eventually, after reaching the opposite side of the gateway with the lamp, your mind will have been decided on the next course of action. It may be quite simple to move the light back to the rabbit that you want to try for first and then slip the dog, or it may be that you have decided that where the rabbits are positioned tonight you need to get to a different spot in the field before slipping the dog to give yourself a better chance of success. Sometimes it may even pay to slip the dog and then run to this preferred vantage point at the same time as your dog is running the other way. Every run will be different; whatever it takes to bring a successful conclusion to the run is what we must do.

At times you may know that there is a slight brow (mound) in the field, and in order to keep the rabbit illuminated if it goes that way you know where you need to get to. Some fields have a depression right next to the hedge; these create a challenge for the dog as the rabbits, when being run, will constantly appear and then disappear into the shadows again just as fast, before reappearing further along. If ever you get the opportunity to watch a dog on its rabbit from the other end of the beam, you will wonder how on earth they ever catch anything. For us, maybe six foot tall, looking directly down the beam, everything is crystal clear; for our dogs, just two foot tall, often looking back up the beam or at best across it, all they often have to aim for is a shadowy silhouette, whilst all the time adjusting their feet and body shape. I once had someone come out and video one of my dogs, to watch later in slow-motion. When it zoomed in on the dog, it was extraordinary: I saw all the minor adjustments she made that on normal occasions would have gone completely unnoticed. One other particularly striking feature and revelation was that not at any time did her eyes leave the rabbit – they were completely locked in to her target. It really was a formidable sight and helped me appreciate even more the effort the dogs put in.

When your dog has concluded a run, when to turn the light out? If the run has been unsuccessful, then as soon as you accept it is a miss, extinguish the light, and providing you have kept up insisting on an immediate return at the end of each run, your dog will eventually learn that as soon as the lamp goes off it must come straight back. This can only be achieved when your dog has learnt it is not a sin to miss a rabbit – you are on the same side and this is part of the night. I have actually seen people punish their dogs for missing a rabbit, believing that this will make it try harder next time. There is no hope for those people, and we can only pity their poor dogs. Those people will never get full enjoyment from our sport or ever build a relationship with their dogs, nor do they deserve to. The dogs, however, deserve so much better.

Should the run conclude successfully and is close, you will see when the dog has things under control. As soon as it has, switch out the light and allow the retrieve to take place in darkness. Should the catch take place at distance, your dog may have, for example, just one leg in its mouth; at these times, we can't see clearly. I always want to help the dog, so at such times I choose to leave the light on until I know it is on its way back. As soon as your dog's eyes light up reflecting from the lamp, you can be sure its head is lifted, so that can only mean it has everything once again under control, so we can confidently switch off the lamp and expect a successful retrieve to take place in darkness.

Other things to bear in mind when a dog is running at distance from you would include the frequent occasions, particularly as your dog becomes more advanced, where you may actually be unsighted of the rabbit due to the range at which the run is taking place; in such circumstances, I lamp the dog, working on the principle that if I can see the dog where the dog actually is, the beam of light will be so much wider that the dog will almost certainly be able to see the rabbit, even though I can't. It is during times such as these that white markings on your dog come to the fore and prove to be a godsend. If you should hear the rabbit squeal, resist the temptation – believing the run to have been concluded – of turning the light off just for a moment until once again you see your dog's eyes light up. Very often rabbits will squeal just prior to being caught; if you mistake this for a catch having actually been made, turning off the lamp at this precise moment could tip the balance of control and in that moment of confusion the rabbit may take full advantage, making good its escape. As before, when your dog's eyes light up, you can rest assured this is never going to be allowed to happen and all is well.

There will be occasions where, through various unavoidable circumstances, whilst on a run the dog gets led out of our sight in some undulating areas. This may happen quite frequently, despite all our best-laid plans to avoid it. Do not think that this is the end of the run; particularly with experienced dogs, all you can do is wait, hope and be momentarily redundant (a kind description for being useless). Very often a catch will still be made. It never ceases to amaze me how frequently old hands succeed under these seemingly impossible conditions, but they do; all we can do is take a break, rely on our dog and let our partner do its thing.

Another regular occurrence when you will need to leave the light on and allow things to develop, unlike the previous example, could happen at any range; it could even happen practically right beside you. A run will seemingly have been concluded and unsuccessful, except, unlike usual moments like these, your dog will not instantly return to you; instead, it will be staring at the hedge. It may even be taking short hops; its tail will be raised and wagging furiously, as it can still hear the rabbit within the hedge. This fact alone indicates to us that the rabbit is not in the part of the hedge that it wanted to be in; in its desperation to find refuge, it has gone in at the nearest point available to it, but this point clearly doesn't offer it the full escape route it was looking for and now it is in a very precarious position. It will be creeping along inside the hedge, destined for somewhere it knows to be safer, but our dog can hear it, and one of three things are likely to happen, and at this precise moment there is no way of predicting which one will prevail. Perhaps the rabbit will indeed find what it is looking for and any chance of a catch goes with it; or your dog will dive into the hedge as soon as it feels sure about the rabbit's exact whereabouts and make a catch when all had originally appeared lost; or your dog will misjudge its dive into the hedge, but yet invariably be close enough to spook the rabbit, which will then bolt back into the field and the run is back on – this run will almost certainly now end with a catch. The time it takes for these incidents to unfold is seconds rather than minutes, but be patient and be ready for them when they occur. I would be confident to say they definitely will happen to you at some time. I would also say that by quite a margin they are more likely to end favourably for you.

As time passes and your dog has started to really piece it all together, it will start to use the lamp in the same way as we do. As you move the beam around the field, glance down at the dog's head and it will be seen to be moving in perfect synchronisation with the lamp, as if the two were in some way connected; pause, and you will see an immediate increased level of alertness, your dog believing that you have spotted something. Alternatively, sometimes while you are scanning you may feel the lead tighten and realise that your dog is now actually spotting rabbits that you had overlooked. You are working together.

When this stage is reached, do spare a thought for all those braggers who started their pups at six months old, having put no effort in at all – by now, unfortunately, they can't even get their dog to return to them. Let them try and fail to correct their self-inflicted problems whilst you are living the dream. But genuinely spare a thought for their poor dogs.

With this level of understanding evolving between both you and your dog and the dog and what you are doing, providing that you have retained all the basic obedience you instilled earlier, you can really start forging ahead.

I always use a slip lead no matter how experienced the dog I am working with might be; that is how we operate. This insistence of choice no doubt speeds up the process of the dog using the light in the way previously described, as it knows no other than to be positioned looking firmly down the beam. With a slip lead you retain complete control on both the moment each run commences and which runs are selected. Some people believe that when their dog gets to a certain stage of competence they can dispense with the slip lead. I know, because I was once one of their number. It is a mistake, and in taking this attitude you are guilty of relaxing your efforts. It is easier to not use a lead, but are we going for ease or are we trying to catch large numbers of rabbits? Have we given up in trying to perfect our craft? We would not like our dog to take its foot off the pedal, so we must be prepared to play our part and also remain focussed in this two-sided team arrangement. By keeping disciplined in the use of the slip lead, if a rabbit is spotted in a less than favourable place than we would ideally like, we can move ourselves to improve our chances of success before slipping the dog. People will claim that their dog won't run until told to; well, I would challenge that and say it may not run until told to, but if its heart is in the job, on spotting a rabbit it will not run until told not to either. That means, often on a quiet night in close proximity to your targets that live constantly on a knife edge of alertness, those few whispered words can make the difference between success and failure. Dog on slip, you instantly readjust to each situation. No words: your dog is right with you; it will have become so accustomed to your ways it will know exactly what is happening and will be ready to play its part when released.

This desirable balance of working together has to be achieved and experienced to fully understand the feelings derived from it; your dog will grow to trust you, due in no small part to the consistent manner in which you tackle and deal with whatever occurs. Never abuse that trust. You will find that you will reach a stage where you will no longer need to wait until your dog has seen a rabbit that you have spotted, and by releasing the lead and hissing, your dog has absolutely no doubt that a rabbit is there and it will run up the beam in anticipation. You will distinctly notice the change in the body language of the dog at the moment it spots the target for the first time. In time, an experienced dog will run extraordinary distances up the beam, never for one second doubting that if you say that there is a rabbit there it will be there.

As your lamping trips grow in number and probably become more frequent, your dog's full range of attributes will be revealed. Each will have their own little ways, and we must accommodate and adapt to complement our partner. Any lamper that remains rigid in his technique, oblivious to the dog he is working with, is never going to get the best from either his sport or his dogs. We all have our own little ways, so why shouldn't the dogs?

Mentality

For me, the biggest and most important attribute a Rabbit Lamping Lurcher could possibly have is an absolute love for what it is doing – the mentality of the dog is so important. All lurchers enjoy Rabbit Lamping, but the good ones really absolutely love it, and nothing can deter them: the weather, the thorns from the hedgerow, injury, nothing affects their strong desire to catch every rabbit they see. When they miss one, you can see that they are frustrated; missing is not part of their make-up or something that they can ever accept. These are the ones with the mentality that we wish for.

Obedience

By training our dogs as described earlier in the book, we have given ourselves the opportunity to take full advantage of the dog's natural abilities; by channelling its actions in the right way, everything that can be done has been done. All the little things that could cost us opportunities of catches in the future have been ironed out and everything to make sure the dog works as fast and as efficient as possible have been instilled.

Picking-Up/Strike

Picking-up ability, of course, is crucial. We often term it as strike rate, and again all Lurchers achieve it to some degree, but some are far more adept at it than others. Some dogs will make several attempts at securing their target; others routinely just one. Some dogs seem to take an eternity to get themselves into a position to make a strike; others will instinctively seem to know how to play it – they will pressure their rabbit into an early mistake, and when that mistake is made, they will immediately take full advantage of the opportunity. Some dogs run with their head held higher than others; my preference is to see a dog with its head down low. Logic tells us that with its head held low, our dog's required reaction time is considerably shortened. Again, the better dogs soon seem to work this out and will run with their head higher in the early part of the run, no doubt aiding visibility, before lowering their head when closing in on their target in preparation for their "strike".

Agility

Agility is always important, but more so for the dogs which perhaps don't have the best picking-up abilities. These dogs, which might take three or four attempts before securing their target, will need to rely on their agility to help them get back on terms with their rabbit in order that they may try again. Rabbits are tricky customers and don't just surrender, so at times even the very best dogs will need to use their agility to help them succeed. On such occasions, we have so much to thank our dogs' Whippet ancestry for.

Hedgerows

Hedgerows, particularly in places like here in Devon, can literally be eight foot wide. We need a dog that will throw itself into it to prevent an escaping rabbit; a dog that pulls up at a hedge is going to severely restrict the night's bag. In areas such as this, Collie-crosses, to give them their full credit, appear to be able to do this well, and not only that, they appear to usually come out of it at the end of the night completely unmarked. However, I have to say that I have also had Collie-crosses that, for me, prove that they carry too much Collie blood by literally shepherding the rabbits away from the hedge, instinctively getting between the rabbit and the hedge, and not making any attempt to actually pick up the rabbit in the early stages of a run, intent as they are on keeping it away from refuge. After being successful with this frustrating method for what they deem to be an appropriate amount of time, as the rabbit tires they then make their move, come out and pick-up the rabbit with ease.

As commendable as this may initially sound, the whole process takes far too long, uses up way too much battery power and way too much of the dog's energy. This frustrating trait has in no small way helped contribute to my preference for avoiding too much Collie blood in our dogs, while, of course, still remaining grateful for the benefits that we do acquire by including the Collie in our mix, but in a much more diluted degree.

Speed

The full speed of your dog, now that it is becoming fully fit, will start to reveal itself. The faster the dog, the better it is for us, but only if it does not come at the expense of agility. We want a fast dog to get to its intended targets as quickly as possible – that goes without saying – but what we also want is that when that rabbit inevitably turns, our dog will remain not far from its tail. A fast dog without agility (or experience) will overshoot its rabbit by such a margin that when the rabbit turns, the time the dog takes to turn and get back on terms with it is too long; the rabbit, finding itself under no immediate pressure to hurry, will slow right down and hop carefully into safety trouble free. That is not what we are hoping for; what we need is a fast dog, of course, but one that will learn to anticipate the ways of rabbits and the actions that they will almost certainly make; then, having done so when required, it will have the physical ability to turn quickly, thus never allowing a large enough gap to develop between itself and its target for the rabbit to feel unpressured. A dog with average or less than average picking-up ability must achieve these situations routinely as a minimum, or its catches are otherwise going to be agonisingly restricted.

The better and perhaps more experienced dogs will, of course, initially use their speed to get on terms with their rabbit; when this happens, should the run's course take it across your line of view, you will easily be able to see how quickly the gap between pursued and pursuer closes. Having now got on terms with their rabbit, you will then also easily notice how the dog uses its sense and perhaps experience to hold back, the gap ceases to close and the dog's head lowers (into "strike" mode). This clever dog knows that it is in exactly the right place to pressurise the rabbit into being uncomfortable and feeling that it needs to turn in, attempting to throw off its pursuer. The problem that the rabbit realises it has is that our dog knows it – this has all been worked out. Our dog has this situation firmly under control. The rabbit's nerve predictably gives, it turns, and with one accurate strike, another rabbit is in the bag. We cannot train the dogs to perform like this, but by the sheer amount of times we take them out, we can perhaps increase the chances of them learning it. However, the better dogs just instinctively do it, and what is more, in doing it they invariably make it look ridiculously simple.

There will be many times during the course of any night's lamping where we will need our dog to be equipped with the necessary speed to cover a considerable distance just to get up to its rabbit. It goes without saying that the faster the dog is at times like this, the better equipped it is to carry out what we require it to do. We can have the most agile dog in the world, but if it doesn't have the speed to get itself into position to use its agility, it becomes no advantage to us; equally, we could have the fastest dog, but if it isn't blessed with the agility to see the job through having got itself into position, then the former becomes no advantage either, so it can be seen how difficult and how important our almost impossible task of acquiring the correct balance becomes.

Squatters

Eventually, we will reach the stage where we believe our dogs are ready to start attempting to take squatters. As the name suggests, this is the art of taking a rabbit intent on freezing to remain undetected from the very seat in which it has decided to stay put. The benefits of taking squatters for any lamper intent on catching high numbers of rabbits cannot be exaggerated; a dog that carries out this discipline well will increase the bag no end, perhaps even by as much as a third on some nights. The primary reason for this substantial increase is due in no small part to the minimal energy that the dog expends in picking-up these squatters; with a dog that has energy to spare, you are at liberty to extend your lamping session, and anything that makes that possible demands to be taken seriously.

Over the years I have tried all manner of different ways of introducing the taking of squatters, before coming to realise that the best, the quickest and the easiest way is to literally not do it at all. Of course that sounds nonsensical, I know, but the reality is, until you feel that your dog is completely ready to take this important step, delay even trying it; instead, restrict your runs to moving targets only. If you are confronted by a squatter before you feel your dog is ready, keep the dog on the slip and walk towards the rabbit, hissing your normal sound to let your dog be certain that a rabbit is definitely close by, until eventually the rabbit bolts for home. Every time that you do this, the dog is learning all the while that the shape you have illuminated in the centre of the light's circle is exactly what you are both after. You will know when the penny has dropped, as the pressure on the lead will leave you in no doubt; but don't be in a hurry to let the dog try for one, no matter how close to the target you manage to get: any failed attempt is an unnecessary small step back, and remember, squat rabbits have not expended their energy. Should a young dog grab one – and it is quite likely under the right circumstances it could – it then has to contend with a strong, fresh rabbit, full of energy and not at all happy about the situation it finds itself in. The obvious and understandable thing to happen would be for the dog to grip tighter; determined as it will be not to lose its catch, its inexperience has not equipped it to deal with such awkward situations, and potentially our impatience has sown the seed of a problem. If we put our dog into situations that may encourage it to grip tighter, it will soon learn that if it does that and the rabbit stops struggling, it becomes so much easier to carry. We do not want our dogs harbouring thoughts like that. We must wait until our dog has learnt how to deal with rabbits and has also learnt how to carry them in a balanced way. Having thus far only dealt with moving targets, when making a catch in these situations, much of the rabbit's limited energy has already been exhausted, and in this condition they become much easier adversaries for a young, relatively inexperienced dog to control.

For the full period that we are resisting the temptation of letting the dog try for a squatter, our dog is learning all the while and now having confirmed in its own mind that this shape in the middle of the light is indeed a rabbit. When we do eventually decide the time is right to try for one, it does not come as a surprise when the dog rushes in and easily picks-up its first squatter at the first attempt. This is not a foregone conclusion, but it is highly likely that this will happen. Sometimes you will get a rabbit that is unsure as to whether it should bolt for home or, in fact, sit tight: moving slowly to one side, then the other, before finally settling on the latter idea to stay put. Should one of these rabbits fortuitously present itself at the right time, it has helped us no end. First of all, it has confirmed to the dog what it is, and now, having done us that enormous favour, it has decided to nestle down in the grass, intending to go unnoticed, which it has already completely failed to do. The pressure on the lead tells us that this rabbit's game is up. As careful as we might be, it is still not impossible that the dog may have made a mistake; it may have focused its gaze on something else it has noticed in the beam – a stone or clod of earth, for example – and when you slip the dog, it runs right past the rabbit. Don't panic, stay calm, all is definitely not lost. As the dog passes, hopefully the rabbit will stay where it is. It is probable that this will happen. Turn off your lamp just for a brief few seconds; when you put it back on, have it shining on the ground right in front of you. As you slowly raise the circle so that the rabbit is just inside the top perimeter of the circle as you look at it, you should also see the familiar sight of your dog's eyes light up in the shadows behind the rabbit, as by now it is so familiar for your dog to come back when the light goes out that when you did put the light out, it will have instinctively turned around. Keep the light where it is and just watch for a while; let things unfold on their own. Your dog will be concentrating, so if the rabbit bolts it will be seen immediately and a normal run will resume, no damage done. You can try for a different squatter on another occasion. The more likely scenario is that your dog will come back towards you, looking intently at the ground for what it strongly suspects is there to be found. If necessary, you can steer your dog into the target by moving the circle of light appropriately; when doing this, you will notice your dog divert its gaze to where the light takes it. When you are certain that the moment is right, instruct your dog to "stay" and move the lamp up so that now the rabbit is in the middle of the circle. Your dog will be looking at a much smaller area of illuminated ground in front of it now, as much of the circle will be behind it, and at last your dog should eventually see the target. If it doesn't, that does not matter. Leave your dog where it stands and move in and bolt the rabbit. Try again another night. Whether your dog takes it from the squat or not, doesn't really matter. If it does, happy days; if it doesn't, the normal run ensues, and nothing at all has been lost. I love intense moments like these. Yes, of course they can go wrong, and it is disappointing when they do, but when they lead to success it feels so good. Seeing the dog that you have trained from a puppy, or perhaps even bred yourself, behaving exactly how you always hoped that eventually one day it might, is extremely gratifying and something we can take great pride in.

Different dogs will show different techniques in dealing with squatters; as long as they work, that is fine by me. My preferred choice is a dog that literally just rushes in and snaps the rabbit up. Simple, efficient and as effective as it is possible to be. Others will go out to the side and come in slower from an angle; again, fine by me, but taking squatters is yet another of the areas where a dog with too strong a dose of Collie can once again frustrate. I have had first-cross Collie-crosses that instead of getting in and getting the job done, when released start stalking in creeping up the beam whilst giving the rabbit the Collie "eye". Even if they did this at a reasonable pace, it would not be so bad, but they often don't. I had one in particular that springs to mind which you could literally walk right past and overtake as she very, very slowly stalked up the beam towards a squatter. That is beyond acceptable, as the time and battery power this takes is just not practical at any time, but particularly if there are other rabbits close by that you desperately want to move onto. A good dog will run up the beam from any distance and snap a rabbit out of its seat, and in doing so is an absolute sight to behold.

Stamina

Being worked regularly and having become fit, our dog's stamina is now called upon to enable it to sustain its nightly exertions. There is absolutely no way of telling what stamina our dog has been blessed with until we reach this point. The importance of stamina will dictate the true value of our canine partner, but only when simultaneously assessed alongside our dog's other attributes. A dog that struggles to pick-up its rabbits but has endless stamina could perhaps equal any particular night's achievements of a far more skilled dog that whilst catching fast and frequently, quickly runs out of energy – the same number of rabbits could be caught by each, just the time it takes would be extended. Time spent out is never a problem, but again it can be seen that it is crucial to secure the right balance of attributes.

At all times in a night's lamping, the handler must be aware of and constantly assessing the dog's ability to continue with the night's exertions; you can be absolutely certain that the dog itself will neither want nor know when to stop. We must make this call on its behalf.

It doesn't matter about any numbers we are aiming for, any record we are close to breaking, any pressure that anybody else with us may apply – the only thing that matters is the dog, and by now you should understand your dog well enough to know when the time is right to make this important decision.

I am speaking from experience, and I am ashamed to say that I have run a dog to exhaustion. It was many years ago now, but I didn't heed the warning signs and in my greed pushed her and pushed her until, eventually, she literally collapsed and had a fit. I carried her home and was very lucky that she survived. I learnt a lesson that night that was to be never forgotten, and I pledged never to be so stupid and selfish again, and have never nor will ever break that pledge: our dogs deserve so much better from us.

If you fear your dog is slowing down, is not returning as quickly as has become the norm, or is perhaps taking longer to recover from its runs, be careful and watch carefully – it is nearly time to go home. If I reach this stage, I call it a night. I have long since worried about chasing my own self-inflicted targets and personal records: I couldn't even carry them now if I caught them, being the dinosaur that I am. If this stage is reached, stop.

Having called it a night, it will be a good time to gut (remove the entrails) the catch; this time taken will also provide your dog with a well-deserved breather. My dogs always get the liver from the last rabbit to be gutted. I have always done this; they always enjoy it and the butchers are unlucky with that one because it's the way it is. If you have stopped because of concerns for your dog's welfare, this morsel will have a rejuvenating effect and perhaps is more appreciated than usual. That definitely does not mean you should continue with your night, but I would recommend offering it as a treat at this particular moment, even if you don't normally.

Incidentally, remembering the night that my dog's lamping session was filmed, the cameraman was extremely conscientious and recorded everything that happened right to the very end of the night. Later, when watching it, I was surprised to see that the bitch that we had out with us – who could be seen throughout this sequence back in the shadows behind me – watched intently from a distance as I gutted the rabbits, only to step forward as I picked up the last one, knowing full well what was about to happen. I never knew that she did that, but I really enjoyed seeing it and realised then that it had, in fact, become expected and was a ritual. I make a point of never throwing this liver to my dogs – they feed from my hand. They are my partners.

Dogs that are out of breath by having several quick consecutive runs should not be mistaken for dogs that are exhausted; give them a minute to get their tongues back in, perhaps before going in to the next field, and they will be fine. When it takes longer than it should for them to regain their breath, start assessing their condition more carefully.

I have deliberately gone through the different attributes that we look for in our Rabbit Lamping Lurchers in order of importance as I see it; this, of course, is through a Devonian's eyes. If you are working your dogs in other parts of the country on different terrain, your list will be exactly the same, but your priorities may well differ. Everyone must interpret their own situations accordingly. My list in descending order of priority is:

Mentality, Obedience, Picking-up, Agility, Hedgerows, Speed, Squatters, Stamina.

From this list of eight attributes, only one – "Obedience" – do we really have complete control over. Fortunately for us, this is near the top of the list, and if we do get the training right it should make it at least possible to influence, if not preferably maximize, the benefits of all of our dogs' other natural attributes. It can be seen that some possible combinations will complement each other, whereas others may sadly affect our levels of success. For example, a fast dog that excels at picking-up is going to find a lot of situations favourable; unlike a fast dog, which might struggle with picking-up and perhaps is not quite as agile as we would like. This dog is going to need to excel at the hedgerow in order to make up for its other deficiencies. Each dog will probably excel at two or three, be average at two or three, and have weaknesses in two or three of the disciplines listed. It is then up to us to identify our own individual dog's strengths and weaknesses, and having done so, plan our nights accordingly.

Depending on the level of interest that you may have and the amount of ground that may be available to you, it could well be that you have decided to have a team of dogs rather than just a single one. If this is the case, then you will have more options available to you when deciding which individual dog's strengths make it more useful in certain areas, whilst accepting that this very same dog's weaknesses are likely to severely restrict its success elsewhere. Whatever it takes to get the best possible results from our sport is what we must do. The best dogs are obviously those which excel in all disciplines, but these so very rarely come along, we cannot possibly plan for this to happen – just dream.

If you have decided that your interest justifies working with a team of dogs rather than just a single dog, think carefully and plan for the future as well as the present. The last thing you want to do is get more than one dog too soon – take that from a fool who has done it! Learn a bit about your trade, make your mistakes and be better prepared second time around. There are also benefits to you by taking this far more sensible route; yes, we have to accept that whilst we only have one dog we are only ever one injury away from having our nocturnal exploits temporarily curtailed. But by bringing in a second at the same time as the first, or very soon after, they are both going to grow old together; bumper years with two fit, strong dogs will be followed by years of natural degeneration. When our dogs retire, they still need to be cared for, they still take up space and they still take up time; they have earnt all of this and more. We can take care of them at this stage of their lives – it is the very least we can do in return for what they have given us – but we don't want our whole team reaching this stage at the same time. So, being patient initially before adding to your team, whilst seemingly affecting progress in the short term, will undoubtedly, for more than one reason, pay dividends long term. Eventually, if you get bitten by the bug, your team may number three. I would suggest to give more than three dogs more work than they could handle would be beyond the capabilities of most people. We all have other mundane commitments in life to which we must attend, and to keep three dogs working hard you will need to have a lot of ground, a lot of rabbits and be fully committed yourself. Even then, if you can satisfy all of these requirements and manage to avoid any serious injuries, you are still going to find that three dogs are likely to prove more than adequate to cater for your needs.

Our dogs, of course, are ultimately the ones who will decide the level of success we enjoy, but the more you go out, the more you observe and the more you will become familiar with the ways of the rabbit. They are not in any way the most difficult creatures to work out when it comes to effecting our particular sport. We find them out feeding and basically try to catch as many as possible before they can return to safety. Of course, rabbits are much more complex and fascinating than this, but for our particular sport that fairly well sums up the segment of their life-cycle during which we come into contact with them. It is amazing if you stop to consider how rabbits act in such a predictable way; whether they are here in Devon, in the Midlands or Scotland, their manner is identical, and if you are familiar with them in one area there is no need to consider them to be different anywhere else.

When you become familiar with being out at night, you will be able to read the rabbit's body language pretty much at a glance the first time you lamp a new area. As you swing the lamp around, rabbits that have been lamped before will run almost immediately; if this action is coupled with many already in tight proximity to the hedges sat up straight, having been disturbed by the noise of your approach, you will struggle – someone else has over-lamped this population and they have become what we call "lamp shy". On the other hand, if you swing the lamp around and the rabbits are out in numbers, many not taking any notice of the light at all, and those that you pause and dwell on wriggle down into a squat, you are entitled to be encouraged. In places like these we can expect to enjoy good sport, as these rabbits have not seen the lamp before. Most farm rabbit populations will probably be somewhere between these two examples, and now the decisions you – the human side of your person/ dog partnership – make will have a big impact on the night in deciding how best to approach it.

In time, your eyes will pick out a rabbit tucked in at a distance with just a fleeting glance, and yet people unfamiliar with lamping can often not see the very same rabbit even when you tell them where it is. I would love a pound for every time that someone has said, "How on earth did you see that?" I feel certain that anyone else who lamps regularly would have heard that self-same comment on numerous occasions as well.

If you are going to entertain company on your lamping trips, it is very important for you to take charge, and your guest must abide by your rules or not come at all. The most important rule must be the safety of your dog; explain to your guest that your left-hand side is for your dog alone and they must walk on your right. People unfamiliar with walking at night will be tripping up on all manner of things – the last thing we want is for them to accidentally step on our dog's feet. *Visitors right side only*. When you enter a field, you go first every time; there is nothing to see until you get there, so you go first. When your dog is running, if the action looks like it is going to come in close, tell the guest that they must step in behind you if a rabbit comes back up the beam, which they often will. Your dog will allow for you to be there; however, it won't expect someone else to be beside you, so the chances of a collision are unacceptably increased. Your dog could easily get seriously injured if your guest has not tucked in as instructed. If your accomplice has brought a dog or perhaps is even leading another of your own dogs, it must not be permitted to get free at any time under any circumstances, but particularly when the first dog is running a collision in the dark; at the speed they travel, it is not going to end well for either. When a rabbit is caught, ask your accomplice to stand still and you take a couple of steps forward so there is no chance of the second dog trying to get in on what the first has achieved and threaten an otherwise perfect retrieve. If you are with someone else, be sure to pay them the same respect and keep back out of the way when their dog is returning its catch.

You won't realise until someone else comes with you just how fast you travel lamping at night. The few times I have begrudgingly allowed people to accompany me, that is always the gripe that I hear. I travel at the speed that feels right, and if they want to come they must find a way to keep up. I don't mind at all if they choose not to come.

I have often heard people say that so-and-so has got a good dog, it caught x number of rabbits in one night single-handed. This x number of rabbits is more likely to mean to me that Mr So-and-so has found a good place to go with a strong rabbit population. I do not rate a dog by the number of rabbits it catches in any particular night; in fact, this number is totally meaningless in assessing the dog's qualities. A dog could have six runs on good, favourable ground with unlamped rabbits and catch them all, yet the same dog could have six runs on poor, unfavourable ground holding lamp-shy rabbits and catch none of them, or at best perhaps one. So I would not recommend becoming involved in bragging about numbers; it certainly does nothing to determine the better dog. Of course, regarding numbers caught, we all have our own personal most successful nights that we remember with pride. But they are better kept private and I certainly wouldn't read too much into it.

If you are happy that your dog is trying its hardest even when the odds are heavily stacked against it and you know for certain that you have done and are continuing to do everything possible to help it achieve the highest standard possible, nobody anywhere could ask or do more. Personally, I have always preferred to go lamping rabbits alone; as time has gone by, this preference has only ever increased. It is a lovely experience to be alone at night with just your dog for company. I couldn't possibly recommend it to be carried out in any other way.

CHAPTER 8
TAKING CARE OF THE CATCH

Whilst in our determined state of attempting to catch as many rabbits as possible, we must not lose sight of the fact that if we cannot sell our catch, then we have defeated the object of attempting to catch so many. If we are getting paid for our efforts either by the head or in response to an already agreed price, then the sale of the catch may be the icing on the cake, as opposed to the total return for our efforts. Either way, we have a moral obligation to make sure that such a good food source is not wasted.

We have discussed the impact that our dogs may have on the rabbit meat regarding the way they catch them and the subsequent gentle way in which they have been encouraged to do their job during the stage between capture and delivering the rabbit to our hand.

From this point on, we alone are responsible for ensuring each one is cared for respectfully.

Using a bag to carry fresh-caught rabbits is the easy and sensible way to proceed as you catch them, but they must never be left piled in a bag for any length of time: body warmth from the rabbits can soon cause the skin covering the entrails to start turning green – most undesirable. Taken from the bag and braced before being carried over the shoulder will allow them to immediately start to cool; at this time, as they are braced together, hold the rabbit in one hand, belly facing in front of you with the rabbit's head uppermost, and, starting from the middle of the rabbit's belly, run your thumb down the centre of the belly, applying slight pressure towards the back legs. It will be seen that this will rid the carcass of any urine which was already on its way to being ejected.

Care must be taken to ensure that the numbers of rabbits caught don't pile up too excessively on our shoulder, with every possible opportunity taken to hang them up and spread them out on a gate, rail, branch or similar, where they will be safe from predation and can easily be collected later in the night.

At the end of the night, having gathered up the catch, they can all then be individually prepared for paunching. To do so, pierce the skin just below the ribcage right in the centre of the belly and gently – perhaps, if necessary, using your finger as a depth gauge – run the knife down the remainder of the belly to almost the base of the rabbit's tail. If you are uncertain of the exact spot from where to start, the ribcage can easily be felt by hand. As the rabbits are cut in this way, they can be laid out on the grass side by side belly up to prevent any leakages in order to keep both them and ourselves clean.

On the conclusion of cutting each rabbit, the knife can be wiped clean on the wet grass or washed in a close-by puddle or water trough and put away.

Now, by lifting each individual rabbit up and holding them around the shoulders with their back in the palm of your hand, insert two fingers into the top of the stomach. You will feel the largest and firmest pouch within located just below the ribs, being careful to leave the liver, which is situated immediately below the ribs, and above this pouch allow a finger to go around either side and as they close at the back, slowly slide the entrails out. You will find it remarkably simple and will very soon be proficient at it. Finally, make sure you have removed all intestines and yet the liver and kidneys remain within. The kidneys are situated half-way down the stomach cavity, immediately below and either side of the spine. Providing you go smoothly and carefully, they will readily stay in place and their presence, along with the liver, will help improve presentation when you deliver your catch to the butcher.

We know that one liver will be missing, but that's for one special unchallengeable reason.

Having treated all rabbits in this way, you can wash your hands in the trough or nearby stream and the catch is safe from deteriorating. Never leave this job until the morning – it must be done now, as soon as our night is over. The only possible excuse for not attending to it now is if we have to unfortunately go to the vet's, but let's hope that is only very rarely.

In the van we can have a number of interlocking storage baskets, and on returning to the vehicle the rabbits can be laid out in these – single layer only, all with bellies uppermost – and they will continue to cool as we go home. Remember, the last rabbits caught during the session could still be warm, even by the time we arrive home. Arriving home, they can be hung up in a cool covered area and can stay there until the morning.

Some of the catch will probably be sold "in the skin", so all that remains to do with these is to remove the strings and put them back in your Lamping coat ready for next time. Re-lay the rabbits back into the baskets, checking each one for any visible sign of damage or disease either inside the stomach cavity or outside on the body; satisfied that all is well, they are ready for delivery.

Those that are to be skinned for sale or freezing can then be dealt with. The first thing to do is to make sure that you have a clean solid bottom and sided tray to place them in once they have been successfully skinned. Other tools we will need are a knife and a cleaver. Holding the rabbit by one side of the stomach wall, separate the skin from the flesh by simply pulling them apart. It is easy, but take care not to rip the stomach wall; it won't affect the flavor, but it will affect presentation. Separate the skin from the flesh as far as the spine, starting from the middle of the rabbit's belly; having done so, slide your knife between the two, pushing the blade through the skin from the inside, then cut back from the spine to the point where you first started so that you now have two flaps of skin. Taking one in each hand, tear the skin around the remainder of the body so that we have now completely divided the skin into two fairly equal halves. Now, holding the cut edge of each, simultaneously pull the skin towards the respective ends; it will surprise you how simple it is, but do take care to not dislocate any legs by pulling too hard in the wrong direction.

Be sure to keep pressure true and in line with all limbs; dislocated legs will ruin presentation

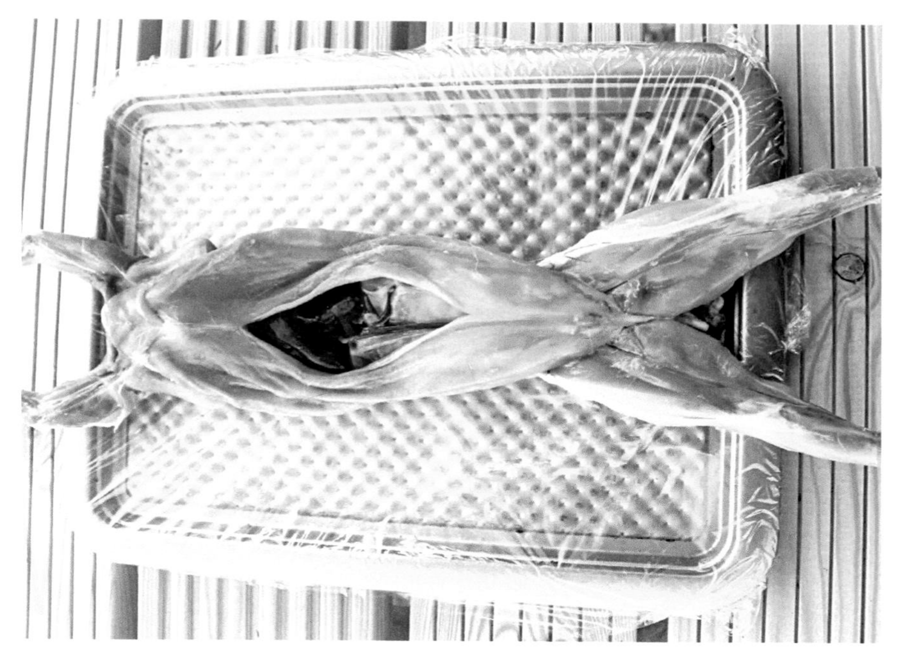

The type of quality that will keep all outlets wanting more

Continue the motion down to the knee joint of the front leg and the hock of the back leg. Holding the body so that the two hocks are together, chop the bottom of the back legs off just on the meat side of where your skinning stopped, let the skin drop to the floor, turn the rabbit around and now carry out the same process with the front legs. Having removed the front legs, adjust the position of the carcass and remove the head at the point where its neck became dislocated. Make sure the tail has come off with the back half of skin; if not, a firm grip, twist and pull will soon take care of that. You should now be left holding a nice, plump, pale pink, immaculate rabbit.

You may notice lines of white fat around the kidneys; that is nothing to be concerned about – it is more an indication that this rabbit lived well.

The whole process of skinning takes much longer to write than to carry out, and you will soon be able to skin a rabbit in this way quite easily in under a minute.

If the rabbits are destined for the freezer, they can now be individually bagged, or if the butcher wanted them delivered skinned, they can be left and delivered as they are. Rabbit sales outlets are an important factor in what we do; time spent in making sure presentation is as good as it possibly can be is never wasted. It is always nice when you walk into the butcher's shop to deliver your catch and a customer that is in the shop just by chance at that particular moment says, "Oh, they look nice"; and while you are dropping them off out at the back, you hear them say that they would like to buy one of the rabbits that just came in. When the butcher comes back to collect it, tell him that one is double the price!

Your efforts have been noticed and not in any way wasted, and though the butcher is most unlikely to admit it or say anything, god forbid your price should go up! He knows he is onto a winner, and you take pleasure from knowing you have got a good permanent outlet for your sales.

CHAPTER 9
BREEDING

Anyone who finds themselves starting to take their Rabbit Lamping seriously is also almost certain to eventually consider the prospect of breeding their own dogs. It has been written, and you will hear it said, that this comes at a cost and it is a lot of hard work. I don't know what these people offering such advice do that makes it this way, because I have bred many litters of Lurchers over the years and have never found it to be either of these things: I have only ever found it to be enjoyable, and whilst never being the motive behind any particular litter, also profitable.

So let's put that to bed right from the start.

This must not mean that we should breed indiscriminately, but equally we should not be deterred from doing what we want to do by others offering poor, unsubstantiated advice. If it was so full of hardship and difficulties, why do they do it themselves?

Your initial search for the right puppy may have proven successful, so in your quest to add to your team you now have various options available to you. One would be to return to the breeder of this first pup and enquire as to whether there may be any plans for further litters of the same breeding in the near future. If there is and you are sure that you are completely satisfied with the dog you have, get your name down for another one from the next litter. Very simple and straightforward.

Alternatively, it might be that whilst being relatively happy with your first dog, you are also aware that it has revealed weaknesses that really need to be improved upon.

Here the two obvious choices need much more careful consideration: the options between looking elsewhere or breeding your own.

Hugely important questions that we must answer first before taking our thoughts of breeding any further include: are these identified weaknesses in your original dog deemed to be minor? Or are they perhaps major? Have these weaknesses been borne through accident or unfortunate experience? Or are they likely to have been hereditary?

Can breeding with this specimen realistically tip the scales in our favour with future offspring, or are we, as I suspect we might be, heading down the wrong road? If a dog has weaknesses, we can accommodate them and adapt ourselves to them whilst we are working so that they have the least possible impact on our sport, as we have already discussed, but I would recommend thinking very, very carefully before breeding from a dog with any prominent weaknesses, regardless of whether they are physical or mental.

The only reason that I would suggest makes any practical sense at all to breed from any dog – or creature, come to that – is when it has proved that it excels at whatever its primary function may be. If in carrying out its intended role it has been found wanting, yes, we could (perhaps) make the necessary improvements with breeding, by carefully choosing the right partner for it, but equally it must be said, and I believe it to be more likely, we may just produce more specimens carrying the same unwanted deficiency. Potentially, if we are not particularly careful in selecting the right mate for our own imperfect specimen, a mate which has proved itself to have strengths in the same areas that our dog has weaknesses, and beyond that one that has a proven track record of being prepotent for these strengths, proving capable of being able to pass them on to its offspring, we may well be opening up a can of worms, incorporating more problems for ourselves and heading on an unwanted downward trend.

If your first dog has proved to have weaknesses and you are sure that they have not resulted from your actions, or anything that has occurred during its lifetime, it is quite likely to be hereditary; not definitely, but unacceptably highly possible. I would recommend enjoying your dog for what it is. Resist the temptation of breeding, but start your search elsewhere for a new pup to add to your team.

There is no point breeding from inferior stock and risking the same problems being perpetuated.

As I wrote earlier in this book, I have had, I believe, only two really outstanding Rabbit Lamping Lurchers in over 40-odd years of Lamping. Both of them were home bred and both of them had very good parents. I have only had a few that I would call "very good", more of what I would class as "good", and plenty that did their best and you could work with them; but only the two really outstanding ones, so using this as an example, it can be seen how rarely they come along. I do not consider that both being bred from "very good" parents was merely coincidence. I think we must learn from that. I do think that I am probably over-critical when assessing my dogs, but I think if we are aiming for perfection we must be honest with ourselves.

We only want to breed from the dogs that have proved themselves to be, at the very minimum, above average, but really concentrate our breeding plans on the outstanding and the very good.

If you are certain that you feel you have a dog that you want to breed from, there is certainly nothing to fear from the process. but do be sure you are doing it for the right reasons.

Season and Mating

Most bitches have seasons once a year; some have two, but the majority just one. The first sign that her season is imminent is quite likely to be that you have noticed that she relieves herself a lot more than usual. Watch carefully, as there is a good chance she is coming into season in a few days' time. You will notice blood on her and almost certainly will notice drops of blood on the kennel floor. Make a note on the calendar –in twelve days' time she is likely to be ready to mate

On the twelfth day, or shortly after, the discharge coming from her will have become practically or even completely clear. Rub your hand down her back firmly and she will probably move her tail to one side: she is ready. Or at least ready to try. Sometimes you will get a mating straight away, but unfortunately some bitches are harder work and need perseverance. Some you may not get a mating until even day nineteen, but that is not common.

Do not try the dog until you are sure the bitch is ready, as if she continually sees him off – which she almost certainly will – by the time she is actually ready he will be half afraid of her reactions and nervous in his efforts.

Before introducing her to the dog, make sure they both have a collar on; this way, when they are tied you can easily supervise the act and neither dog nor bitch is in any increased danger of becoming hurt. Be sure to be comfortable, because sometimes they will remain tied for an extended period. When a bitch has mated, I prefer a repeat mating the following day just as a precaution. Obviously, if you have travelled to the dog, that may not be feasible; but if possible, I would recommend it. If you have used a stud dog belonging to someone else, I would also recommend paying for the service, not agreeing to the dog's owner having pick of the litter – you want first pick. Once a bitch is believed to be in pup, I wouldn't work her after about a fortnight into her pregnancy; by that time in, bitches having a sizeable litter, you may well have already started to see a very slight change. Our breed are not shaped or coated to hide their condition; a more usual size or smaller litter may still not be visible for a further week to ten days.

Preparing for the Birth

The pups will arrive on or near the sixty-third day. Having decided where the pups are to be born, I like to make sure the bitch lives there for at least a week before the pups are due, just to settle in. I use a separate shed away from the other kennels which is quiet and secure; it is divided into two sections, one of which is for bedding and one for food and water. The bedding area is lined and insulated and is equipped with a heat lamp in case it should be required. The bed itself is a rubber mat "borrowed" from a local dairy farm that they use for the cows to lay on in the winter. This is covered with a thin layer of shavings and completed by a generous layer of straw. This keeps the pregnant bitch nice and calm and comfortable in the last few days of her term.

Whelping

Unlike many other breeds, ours tends to have the litters needing minimum assistance. Immediately prior to starting whelping, the bitch is quite likely to appear distressed and vocal; this is quite normal, but it might be worth touching base with your vet just to let him know what is happening and make sure you have the phone number of who is on duty, just in case help is required. If it is your first litter, I think this is of more importance, and despite charging ridiculous prices, in everyday situations most vets will offer help over the phone at a time like this if it is needed. Just prior to birth, the bitch is also quite likely to start digging, sometimes seemingly frantically; again, this is perfectly normal and nothing to worry about. At this time I dispose of most of the bedding. Too much bedding could see a pup burrow into it unknowingly and get overlooked. Soon, you will notice the bitch contracting; this, of course, will hopefully be followed by the first pup. When the pup is born, be ready to help, but don't interfere – a very difficult instruction to fulfil. If the bitch is doing all the right things, sit back and watch.

If she is not biting the sack away from her first pup, intervene and at least get its head out for her; that way we know the pup can breathe, even if mum is a bit slow in getting going. Practically every time after the first pup is born, even with maiden bitches, instinct kicks in and soon mum will be taking charge and will very quickly appear expert at what she is doing. I love these moments; it is a lovely time to enjoy and share with her and I have never felt that my presence has ever been anything but reassuring to the bitch I am watching over.

Gaps between pups being born are of no fixed time; it could be minutes, it could be hours. As the number of pups grows, watch that none get squashed when mum reaches back to attend to either herself or the next puppy being born. Lift them clear and safe without moving them too far from her; when she settles, move them back close to her again. Gradually, the number of pups born will, of course, grow. Lurchers usually have between seven and ten, but that is only a very loose guide. Over the years I have had as few as three in a litter and as many as fourteen. I have heard of litters both smaller and bigger than these numbers, but seven to ten is the norm. The birth of the pups is, as you would expect, quite an ordeal for the bitch, but because you have been present and shared the experience, you will eventually detect a moment when you just feel that the full litter has now, in fact, been born. The bitch will appear comfortable and intent on cleaning her pups and not in any way as tense as she has been, and the noises the pups are making will tell you that they have found where their all-important first feed comes from, and everything about the moment will suggest peace and calm. The litter is born. When the bitch stands up later, as a precaution you can just gently feel her belly to make sure that there are no more puppies within, but nature so rarely gets it wrong.

Pups

For the first few days and nights after birth, I like to check on the pups as regularly as possible, primarily to have a quick head count to make sure no pup has wriggled under – or worse, behind – mum. If at a glance all can be seen to be well, I like to make a fuss of the bitch, but don't touch the pups; this way she just becomes reassured that your visits are nothing to be concerned about and she remains relaxed throughout.

If I could order the number of pups in a litter, I would have six. With this number, the pups prosper without undue competition and with six pups to care for, the bitch is busy without being overly employed. Unfortunately, the choice is not ours to make.

For the first two weeks nothing really changes, other than the pups get bigger. The bitch will be reluctant to leave them at all for the first week, but after that she may enjoy a break. We leave the shed door open so that our bitches can go outside if they want to, but they never take advantage of that for long, soon wanting to return to check on their pups. I tend to encourage the bitch to join me on a short walk at this time; some do, some get to the garden gate and then show you that they don't really want to go. That's fine by me they – call the shots. Eventually they will decide the time is right and then you can gradually extend their exercise in line with how happy they are to continue. It is commonly said that bitches shouldn't be allowed out at this time due to the possibility of picking up a germ and transferring it to their pups. This may or may not be right. I am not in any way qualified to say, but I always let my bitches go out if they want to and my pups have never come to any harm.

At two weeks old the pups receive their first worming dose based on their weight, and through this we get the first true indication of which are the biggest and which are the smallest. Despite still having their eyes closed, if I have a big litter of, say, more than nine pups, I tend to offer them food at this young age. I know that this does not concur with recommended advice you will read on the side of your puppy meal sack, so I am not qualified to tell anyone to do it, but I always do. I feel it gives the pups a boost and, more importantly, it helps the bitch out with her heavy workload. I mix the puppy meal up thoroughly to a consistency of a thick gravy and place the puppies around a shallow dish. They soon get the hang of slurping it up and I have never had any problems from doing this once or twice a day from this age. If the litter is below nine, I tend to leave it to mum; she will cope and can do far better without my help in dealing with this smaller and more manageable number.

Some people will say that they can pick their puppy out as soon as it is born. How that is achieved is beyond me. I watch the pups develop as intensely as most and I can never make a final choice until it is time for the remaining pups to leave, and even then I am often not completely sure that I have picked the right pup. I guess if your requirements are based on sex or the colour of pup, you could choose early, but I never care about either of those factors; it has to be the best pup for me, whatever its sex or colour may be, and my choice frequently goes from one to another as they develop. The better the litter, the harder to choose.

Between two and three weeks the pups' eyes will open and by the end of the third week they will be staggering around. Food can now be provided as recommended on the puppy meal sack, a little often being the key. Don't just drop it down and allow the first ones to find it and take the lion's share; offer it in a receptacle suitable for them all to feed around comfortably. Lift them into place after first evicting mum, who may otherwise eat it all. With a big litter I tend to separate the pups into two equal-numbered groups around two dishes; bigger pups around one and the smaller pups around the other. When you can see they want no more and are satisfied, mum can come in and finish the rest.

At this time I like to set up a second bed for the bitch in the second area of the shed, as by now the pups are getting more boisterous and she will appreciate quiet moments to herself. Make sure that the dividing wall is in no danger of being scaled by a determined "climber"; but despite this precaution, if it should still happen, be sure to take note of which pup the determined "climber" is before making the wall higher again.

At four weeks old the blobs have become real little puppies and are starting to get inquisitive and demanding. The second worming takes place and their weights can now be compared to the first weights recorded at their initial worming. In assessing the progress of each, it will often be seen that their size rankings fluctuate regularly, none of which matters as long as they are all prospering. A small, very shallow drinking bowl of water is provided at this time, which is increased in size accordingly from now on.

At this age I now start to take a more intense interest in their development and record any opinions in a notebook. It is so easy to forget your thoughts as time passes, so I continue this recording until the final selection has been made. I always keep these notebooks, and it makes for interesting reading later when the pup or pups you have kept mature: you can see how much of what was identified at this early stage has transpired, both physical and apparent mental attributes having been noted.

The pups can now start to explore (wreck) the garden, while mum can return to the kennels for gradually lengthening periods, leading to just returning at nights by five and a half weeks to not returning at all at six and a half weeks. Any family or friends with children may like to visit now – everyone loves puppies, but more importantly, our pups benefit from these socialising periods. We are fortunate where we live to have a secure front garden where the pups can not only play but also experience passing pedestrians and traffic, benefiting from the introduction to both. We also have a dog in our kennel who appears to have appointed himself as chief protector; in addition to this, he also appears to be able to see through brick walls because if anyone dares to stop and look, or god forbid speak to the pups over the gate, he lets the world know that he is not in agreement with their action, which is great for us but perhaps not so much appreciated by our neighbours.

Pups receive their third worming at six weeks old and it may be that whilst you have not chosen the pup(s) you will keep, you have by now identified siblings that will not be retained; these can be made available to others providing you are sure, always making it clear to would-be purchasers the reasons any particular pup is available. It could be that the reason this pup is not for you, for example size, could be the very same reason that it appeals to others. It is nice to have good homes ready for the unselected pups when they reach eight weeks so that you can focus your undivided attention on your own selection.

Six and a half weeks through to eight weeks is really just about making sure that the pups are completely self-sufficient now that mum is not caring for them any longer. Making sure that every corner of the garden has been thoroughly destroyed, fighting with brothers and sisters, eating ever-increasing amounts of food and sleeping, but in no particular order. Some bitches play with their pups, which is always nice to see; some, although they have been attentive mothers when they needed to be, have now just had enough of the nonsense, and it is nice to give the bitch the opportunity to decide for herself which category she is in.

As with everything connected to breeding Lurchers, it is unfortunately wide open to variation, but as a very rough guide, my records suggest that the pups that should develop into the approximate right size for us would weigh about 2.5 kilos at six weeks old and perhaps a little over 3.5 kilos at eight weeks.

Between seven and eight weeks old, all puppies need to be micro-chipped by your vet by law, and after worming again at the eight-week stage they are now ready to disperse to their new homes.

EPILOGUE

Take a broom handle to a snooker hall and have a few shots with it, and you will almost certainly pot some balls; however, if your interest is such that you wish to improve and perhaps compete with others, you will certainly need to find a cue made for the job. It may not be a very good one or even suit you, but despite these failings your performance will undoubtedly improve. Should you be fortunate enough to find you have a flair to match your interest and a desire to improve even further, then it won't be long before your thoughts will turn to trying to find exactly the right cue to help you accomplish this.

So it is with us and our Rabbit Lamping dogs, and come to that any other pursuit within which someone may try and test themselves; the more effort you put in, the greater your chance of success. But to really succeed you need to have the right tools at your disposal, and for us – though we would never class them as tools – our dogs will be the one fundamental factor which will ultimately determine our level of success. There is not a Lurcher born that could not catch a rabbit on the lamp given the right opportunity; either sex, any colour, any size or any combination of breeds, they will all catch rabbits, and many will catch enough to satisfy the modest requirements of their respective lamping owners. There are those who will scoff at our chosen pursuit and deem it to be unsporting and not in any way a true indication of any dog's working credentials nor worthy of any serious application or consideration. One can only assume that these unfortunate people have never had the good fortune to witness an experienced specialist

Rabbit Lamping dog in action, because if they had and they were true dog men, their opinions would definitely change very quickly.

All Lurchers will catch rabbits – that is a fact. Most will not struggle, given a reasonable level of fitness and average ground, to get into double figures; many will take more, perhaps double or even treble this number, but gradually the dogs not so ideally suited to our sport will be found wanting. The number of runs that they need to be presented with to accomplish these figures proves too much for them and with fatigue playing its part, they will invariably reach the limit of their capabilities. Specialist dogs more suited to the sport who habitually miss far fewer runs and pick-up their quarry much quicker than their less-suited counterparts, and in doing so saving that all-so-valuable energy, will, given the opportunity under the same circumstances, quickly surpass the efforts of those not so naturally equipped. Argue as much as you like in defence of whatever types of dogs you prefer, these are, like it or not, the simple facts. You do get exceptions; we have already covered that should you be blessed with one of those you are very, very fortunate, but you should not expect one, because they will only come along very, very rarely, if at all.

As important as the right dog undoubtedly is, having secured one this, of course, only represents fifty percent of the team. We, the handlers, have a massive part to play if we want to achieve the best possible results. How many times have we been confronted with a situation where if we entered a field via the open gate we are standing beside we know there will be rabbits, but we also know that they will be difficult for the dog to catch when approached from this particular direction? There is another gate into the same field from which we should enter to stand a much better chance of success, but that means an additional quarter of a mile walk to get there. If we are inclined to take the former option and just hope for the best, I suspect each night's tally will be detrimentally affected by our application. Should we be inclined to take the latter option without even thinking twice, then this would perhaps suggest that we may have the right level of determination to succeed and are clearly better equipped as handlers to play our part.

As a Gamekeeper, each season it fell upon me to assemble a team of pickers-up for our shoot days. At times you were in a situation where beggars couldn't be choosers, but during times when there was a surplus of candidates from which to choose, it became interesting to evaluate people and their dogs for the job intended; of course, always carried out privately. So often you would find good dogs coupled with less desirable handlers and, vice versa, really useful people with sub-standard dogs. Good dogs with handlers who were prepared to put themselves out over a sustained period in all weathers proved few and far between. Attending to this duty reinforced my already-held opinion of how equally important both dog and handler are – not individually, but more importantly, when evaluated and considered as a pair. In our world the right pairing is still no guarantee of high numbers of rabbits being caught if the quarry is not available to us, but it will certainly ensure a high level of success on those that are. Again, with the pickers-up you will see the person burdened with carriers full of birds turning up at the game cart five minutes after the drive has concluded, having gathered birds from around the guns' feet – birds you don't even really need a dog to collect, taking all the plaudits from those that know no better and have more money than sense. Much later, as the majority of soup cups are being cleared away, you see someone else who has been picking-up at the back arriving with far fewer birds; but each one having been difficult to recover, I guarantee it will be this person who will be seen rubbing his dog down with a towel, before offering it a light meal and a drink of fresh water, with a nice clean bed of straw to lie in, before the handler goes into the shoot lodge for his/her dinner at the end of the day. Inside the shoot lodge, he/she will quite likely find the former already on dessert, with his/her shivering dog unattended in the back of a cold truck. I know which one I want in my team and I know which one I would like to think I would be in similar circumstances.

How often we wish we knew when we were younger what we have since learnt later in life. When I remember my early seasons as a Rabbit Lamper, given the equipment I used, the tactics I employed and the general way I went about it, I can only marvel at the dogs which accompanied me during those formative years, as any success was purely down to them; despite being burdened with me, they still turned a night's sport into something that was at that time considered to have been some sort of success, and no doubt in my mind I very wrongly believed that most of the credit for it lay with me.

Having started lamping rabbits as an incredibly enthusiastic "entertainment lamper", which eventually and somewhat predictably evolved into becoming an extremely "serious lamper", perhaps even bordering on an obsessed lamper, I later became a Gamekeeper. Now I appear, without any pre-planning, to have gone full circle and once again become at best an entertainment lamper. When I am out, I feel that my mind still thinks as a serious lamper's would, but in reality my time of staying out lamping rabbits all night, night after night after night in all weathers are behind me; being a dinosaur, it is doubtful I could even carry the catch like I used to if I tried.

For Rumour, though, she is now ready and prepared to start her working life. It would be most unfair for me to ever consider comparing her to dogs that I have worked with in the past; they had so much more opportunity to hone their skills, and in doing so become so proficient in what they did. She will, however, definitely get her chance to make her mark and will no doubt benefit from the protection created by my previous experiences that my unfortunate earlier dogs had to sadly work their way through and find a way past.

If only I could find a way to wind back the years!

I hope that within these pages information can be found that will help people get off on the right foot and not make all the so easily avoidable daft mistakes that I have made, both in technique and choice of canine partner. I knew no better. Now, after so many years of practical experience, I feel that perhaps my struggles and experiences documented here could prove useful to others either just starting out or indeed perhaps as an alternative view to one already established. It is certainly not suggested that this is the "be all and end all" because, despite lamping for as long as I have, I still continue to see things happen that I have never seen before and continue to learn all the time. Life, unfortunately, is simply not long enough for any of us to know it all.